AGAINST THE GRAIN

A Married Woman's Unprecedented
Journey into the Film Industry

SHWETHA SRIVATSAV

STARDOM BOOKS

www.StardomBooks.com

STARDOM BOOKS
112 Bordeaux Ct.
Coppell, TX 75019, USA

Copyright © 2024 by Shwetha Srivatsav

All rights reserved. No part of this book may be reproduced or used in any manner without written permission of the copyright owner except for the use of quotations in a book review.

FIRST EDITION AUGUST 2024

STARDOM BOOKS, LLC.
112 Bordeaux Ct. Coppell, TX 75019, USA

www.stardombooks.com

Stardom Books, United States
Stardom Alliance, India

The author and publishers have made all reasonable efforts to contact copyright-holders for permission, and apologize for any omissions or errors in the form of credits given. Corrections may be made to future editions.

AGAINST THE GRAIN
A Married Woman's Unprecedented Journey Into the Film Industry

Shwetha Srivatsav

Pg. 121
13.97 x 21.59

Category: PER004000/Performing Arts : Film & Video - General
SEL021000/Self-Help : Motivational & Inspirational

ISBN: 978-1-957456-53-9

DEDICATION

To my cherished family, your steadfast support has been my rock, and to all my well-wishers, your encouragement has fueled my passion. This book is a tribute to the love and inspiration I've received from each of you and for all the people out there who believe in equality rights.

ACKNOWLEDGMENTS

Every individual carries within them a unique narrative, whether it's their own or someone else's. Some tales are marked by tragedy, others are deeply relatable, and a few are cloaked in mystery. Then, there are the rare stories like mine, seemingly impossible yet waiting to be unveiled here.

The essence of sharing experiences, inspiring, and motivating one another is the heartbeat of our existence. It is this very essence that I aim to encapsulate in my writing. While I may not have initially aspired to be an author, the necessity to pen down my journey became undeniable. Sadly, in a society still dominated by patriarchal norms, even the remarkable achievement of a married woman like me was often overlooked. Through this book, I seek to challenge these narratives and redefine what constitutes true accomplishment.

For the past two decades, achieving what others deemed impossible – entering into the limelight as a lead actor or starting a career in the mainstream film industry after marriage – has been my reality. Yet, there's no pride or joy in proclaiming this feat when it remains an anomaly. Instead, it leaves me questioning why such milestones for women are not commonplace in our society or the film industry.

Why do married women continue to hesitate or feel reluctant to pursue careers in entertainment after their marriage? Is the issue rooted in the industry, societal norms, or within women themselves? These unanswered questions, coupled with my own experiences, have ignited a fire within me to share my story through this book. It's time to challenge the status quo and pave the way for a more inclusive and empowering future.

ABOUT THE AUTHOR

Mrs. Shwetha Srivatsav, a prominent South Indian film actress, who passionately advocates for the women's rights and equality, dedicating herself through her work in films to empower women and champion their growth and justice. Her voice resonates strongly in the pursuit of women's welfare, both on and off the screen.

Shwetha Srivatsav has completed her post-graduation degree, M.S. in Mass Communication, from Bangalore University. She shattered barriers by becoming the first married woman to play lead in commercial films in the Kannada film industry, and she did not just limit herself to art movies. This groundbreaking achievement came after years of waiting for opportunities, spanning two decades where it was unheard of for a married women to pursue lead roles in mainstream cinema. Undeterred by societal norms, Shwetha defied expectations with sheer determination and talent, fearlessly embracing lead protagonist roles that garnered acclaim and recognition throughout the South Indian film industry. Her performances resonate with strength and empowerment, leaving an indelible mark on audiences.

Hailing from a rich theatre background, participated in numerous stage plays and theatre groups. Honoured to be a proud disciple of the legendary B.V. Karanth and Mrs. Prema Karanth. During her college days, Shwetha worked as an assistant editor for the Kannada theatre magazine 'EE-Masa Nataka, founded and run by her father, L. Krishanappa.

Beyond her cinematic achievements, Shwetha being a two-time Filmfare Award winner in the Best Actor – Female category, demonstrates a profound commitment to philanthropy. She channels her passion towards initiatives such as saving the girl-child, promoting sustainable living, and supporting numerous animal welfare organizations, viewing it as her social responsibility. She wholeheartedly dedicates herself to charitable endeavours, relentlessly striving to make a significant and positive impact in every capacity possible.

Despite the demands of motherhood, Shwetha adeptly balances her career in cinema, social commitments, and family life, earning admiration and popularity for her exceptional ability to manage multiple roles with grace. She continues to take on lead protagonist roles in mainstream cinemas even after embracing motherhood (defying the odds of the Kannada industry's limited market and scarcity of opportunities for female-oriented subjects), successfully she could complete four such projects. Shwetha Srivatsav serves as an inspiration to countless women and girls, embodying the spirit of perseverance and determination. Her journey, marked by hard work and resilience, stands as a testament to what one can achieve without a godfather or a strong support system, navigating the intricacies of the industry with sheer grit and determination, even after marriage. She continues to inspire countless dreamers, igniting their aspirations with her remarkable story of success.

Join Shwetha Srivatsav on an exciting journey through her life, as she shares behind-the-scenes moments and exclusive sneak peeks to personal updates and interactive sessions with fans.

Stay tuned for the latest news, projects, and glimpses into the world of Shwetha Srivatsav.

@SHWETHASRIVATSAV

CONTENTS

1.	MIRROR	1
2.	MAKEUP YOUR MIND, GIRL!	11
3.	STORYBOOK	19
4.	ALARM	29
5.	ROSES & THORNS	37
6.	UMBRELLA	47
7.	STARDOM	57
8.	CHANGING DIAPERS	67
9.	IF I WERE A BOY	75
10.	SWITCH	89
	QUESTIONS and ANSWERS	97

1
MIRROR

Woke up to see the most beautiful sight—yes, my 5-year-old daughter right beside me, with a half-smiling face staring right into my eyes! It was a comforting and a gorgeous morning. My better half, who was up early and busy steaming the water for me. I start my day with a glass of warm water, followed by my affirmations filled with gratitude. Am I this 'Law of Attraction' believer kind of a person?!! All I can say is that I'm just a 'believer.' A belief system is something that helps us to have faith in ourselves. In this book, I will be spilling a lot about myself, irrespective of whether it is a tiny matter to me or a significant challenge/hurdle encountered where I'm very keen to tell the world. Everybody wants to share their story, but some stories have to be heard to bring about change in the mindsets of society, and such is my story. Let's dive into my world then. It was my birthday, and we were on an exotic beach resort holiday with my family. I was living my dream—a free-minded, happy soul, peaceful from deep inside and without inhibitions. Doesn't this sound as if I have achieved it all? No, not yet.... But what is it that is really making me feel so content in my life now? Looking back, I grew up in a low-middle-class family with a very rigid upbringing and hard restrictions on each thing. *"Mommy...mommy, let's cut the cake, I'll blow the candles, mommy!!"* During the breakfast at the resort, before my thoughts could drag me to the depths of the past, I felt tiny little arms wrapping around me, my daughter's arm, and my bundle of joy standing with super excitement. The resort staff arranged a beautiful birthday cake for me. I'm thankful for the nourishing moment in my life. Just then, all this was happening; my hubby reminded me that it was time to click a picture with the birthday cake and share it with the extended family and my well-wishers on social media. They would be curious to know what's happening in our personal lives, which is familiar with celebrities. It means a lot to me, though.

I remember how excited I was for my birthdays as a child. But I never got to celebrate my birthdays at all back then. As we know, it's a day when everyone showered you with attention and love. You could make it special in any way you wanted. Many students from my school would distribute chocolates to the entire class to celebrate the occasion. As kids, we used to look forward to that particular day. Somehow, my father was reluctant to give prominence to such occasions. And I couldn't understand why my father was not happy or excited like other parents are on their children's birthdays. To cover this up, my mother made homemade sweets, and she could do only what was in her control so I could distribute them in my class. It was unusual, and my brother and I were used to doing primarily unusual things compared to others' lives. I never felt my family was normal.

The atmosphere at my house used to be different, making my brother and I fearful, introverted, shy kids. Even when I distributed the sweets among my classmates, I had no confidence, and half of the day was ruined by my insecure feelings, leaving me extremely embarrassed all the time. One fine day, I asked my dad why we couldn't celebrate birthdays like normal families. So, one fine morning, my father was sipping his hot filter coffee while reading the newspaper. He used to sit on the floor near the door to read it in the sunlight, gazing inside the house. Nervously, I approached him with a low voice. *"Appa, for my birthday, I would like to buy a new dress* and chocolates to distribute to my classmates." *By then, almost, my eyes were filled with tears. With low self-esteem.*

"*Hmmm...birthdays aren't special until they are celebrated by others. First, learn to build your personality in such a way that people would want to celebrate YOU and your contribution to society,*" he said to my face in a harsh tone. As a kid, I failed to understand what he was trying to say. Tears couldn't hold back in my eyes, and I ran into the kitchen.

His words were a hundred percent true, but digesting them at our age was difficult for us. Perhaps my father was trying to express that—as a person, what you have contributed to society matters, so people should celebrate your birth rather than follow the norms without any purpose/intent. And I do agree with him now.

I was reminded of my father's lesson. By now, I must have felt deep gratitude toward the people who chose to acknowledge my work and celebrate "me" for my personal and professional successes. But I have outgrown this.

Your birth. Your existence should matter only between you and your consciousness. Everything else is nothing but a 'MAYA.

I always thought my work needed to be aligned with mainstream expectations. I have listened to myself and done what I like. To be loved and appreciated despite treading on the road not taken is a joy I will always cherish in my life. Anyway, what is better for me now is to enjoy my existence with my delightful husband and daughter by my side.

When I see her as young and adorable as ever, I am reminded of how tough being a child can be. I was a shy kid, so there were no surprises there. I was an introvert who had a tough time participating in the world. It was also difficult for me to make friends and communicate with my family members. A dark cloud always loomed over me, stopping me from expressing myself to the world. Growing up, I often wondered what made it so difficult to agree with him now. It was for me to find my voice as a child. In retrospect, it was a sense of inferiority within me. Before anyone else could tell me I was inadequate, I would suggest that to myself, protecting myself from criticism.

As a child, we can all recollect instances of fear, joy, shame, and gratitude that we consciously felt for the first time. These memories shape us, helping us make decisions that could help us find our place in the world. I have always known that my struggles are essential. When I think of these memories, I do not think of them from a place of anger or hurt. I do not think of them from a place of resentment; I look at them as milestones of my journey. I look at them as the detours I had to take to reach here. I view myself from the point of love, from the point of healing. I embrace them. I will open up more about them as we go, but my dear reader, I want you to understand why they are essential.

My journey as an actor and public person has been steep. There were times when the climb took a lot of work and could have been more convenient. However, I have realized that entering the world of cinema was one of the many ways I could overcome my childhood troubles. After all, if learning how to act was like climbing, it certainly helped me climb out of the walls I had built around myself. As a child, my thoughts always roamed in the alley of nothingness. I felt like I had no ambition. I had no drive. I just woke up and got on with my routine. Academically, I was an average student. My world revolved around my family, and my father was my superhero.

Orphaned, deprived of any emotional or financial support from anyone, he raised all of us with utmost love and care. He had been through tough times but ensured we never had to.

He had not met his parents to understand the barebones of parenting. Whatever he did, he did on his own. I wouldn't call him strict. But I will call him a man of principles. My father was a self-made man who never shirked away from his parental role or job in the outer world. While he strived to earn bread for the family, my mother remained a homemaker. She ran the household, cared for our needs, and pampered us with love. I was born into a family struggling to stand on its feet. Nevertheless, we created what we didn't have in money with love.

My father is a renowned theatre personality whose journey has inspired many of them. My brother and I were sent to unique summer camps and theatre workshops as children. I remember these workshops as being my first encounter with acting and performing. Astonishingly, my first encounter with acting was not very comfortable for me. I felt the pressure to perform in an unequal world. Many kids who were a part of the same workshops were very comfortable in their skin. Moreover, they could collaborate and communicate, and I could not.

I could act organically during those theatre workshops despite my circumstances' discouragement. I did not realize it then, but these workshops were preparing me for the future I am living now. Very early in my childhood, I was made to participate in school plays and other drama-related contests.

Shockingly, I wasn't interested in it myself. I didn't have any will to join the theatre group. It felt overwhelming to act in front of an elite crowd then. My inability to express myself was suddenly becoming an obstacle again. My father's efforts to introduce me to theatre performances felt more like a punishment when I found my contemporaries comfortable expressing themselves well. It felt like I was thrown into another den of discomfort. Though I could act better than many, I always preferred to take center stage. I struggled to befriend anyone and was always by myself. Bereft of any desire to perform, I used to sit in the corner, watching everyone. But then, someone else was watching me too—(late)Prema Karanth, ma'am. I never understood how she recognized my talent when I made minimal effort to display it.

Now and then, she used to call my name to come over to the stage. She'd like me to show the other kids how to perform certain characters. My confidence was splintered among those other kids, and Prema Madam seemed relentless in making me take the stage. At that time, all I could think was, "Why me?" But later in my life, I realized that her efforts did bear the sweetest fruits of my success. She was a helping hand, constantly trying to help me overcome my fears. She was an astounding judge of acting and loved all of us equally.

My peers struggled with performing what was told. However, I felt the characters' skin crawl onto me and take over me. I perfected body language sooner than others and could easily memorize stage directions. The shackles of my mind bound me. I did not feel good about myself as I felt different from others. I was too young to appreciate the beauty of differences. If I faltered in my communication skills or realized that my oil-soaked hair was not welcome in a room, I would cripple myself with anxiety and fear. Acting was a gift that walked into my life at a young age, but it took me a while to unwrap it and use it as I do today.

We grew up with strict discipline, and fear breeds within me throughout my childhood. I was always in doubt, not knowing what to do with my life. My parents did try their best to infuse smiles on all our faces. But somehow, I felt my parents were tangled up in societal pressures. There is a reason for it. Now that I am a parent, I understand that the intention behind every rule parents usually put on us is simple: they are trying to protect you. Sometimes, we don't understand it. We resist and rebel, but the intention remains. Even as a 7-year-old girl, I would feel suffocated within the bastion of norms and rules. I love my parents more than anything and will always remain indebted to them for all their sacrifices to raise me. As children, we hardly understand what goes through a parent's mind.

Every parent wants what is suitable for their child. They all want to see their children prosper in life. At the same time, it can never be palatable for a parent if society tags their child as an outcast.

Over the years, I have learned that parents pressure themselves so no one says anything to their children. Sometimes, this pressure also falls upon the children, leading to communication gaps. However, I have learned that we can always overcome these pressures and unite as a family.

Over the years, juggling these roles has become more accessible, and I have been assured that everything can be overcome with time and kindness. My experience as an introverted child made me apprehensive about the world from a very early age. It stole the ability to join the world and be at one with it. All decisions and words became heavy exercises I refrained from undertaking. However, I am so comfortable in my skin today that I have chosen to share my journey with the world. My world revolves around communicating effectively to mark my place as an actor in a competitive industry.

Furthermore, I have tried establishing a genuine and positive connection with my audience. They have looked for me through my work and appreciated me for who I am. These experiences would have been terrifying for a younger me. It's scary how time passes, just like the wind, as cliché as those sounds. Fifteen years ago, I had not imagined my life would turn out like this. Now that I'm fortunate to have seen the best birthdays for three consequent years (just before I took maternity break), my well-wishers/fans flooded my place to catch a glimpse of my birthday/or to meet-greet when my movies were doing great, and my movies were blockbuster hits then.

Also, very early in my career, I witnessed how it all fades away once you are away from the limelight. However, these experiences helped me understand the graph in an actor's life and how to accept it graciously, whether it is a success or a failure. Since childhood, I have encountered many hurdles just for being born as a "girl" in a middle-class family of parents with a problematic mindset and a rigid environment. Today, I'm living my dream. What made me create this world myself were my fights within my mind, my battles with society, and my strength as a girl fighting to attain my fundamental rights.

At the end of my birthday, I was standing in front of a mirror as I had a habit of untangling my hair. If I am in a mood to think, this helps me separate my confusion and clear my mind. A thought provoked me, and I realized that I should be sharing my exceptional journey today with the world of deciding to become a film actor, POST-MARRIAGE indeed, and all the hardships I endured chasing my dreams because of my marital status. Engaging the toddler and enjoying the messy motherhood is part of this crazy journey, too.

Finally, after so many sleepless nights in this journey, seems happy to crash on the bed, and that is when I decided to share my secret to success through this book. Many achievers share their hardships, and we all appreciate that as reaching out for success itself is not easy, but why is my story important or different?

I always acknowledge that even thinking of chasing her dreams and goals seems complicated for a girl (especially those with no financial independence). And once she gets married, half of her life looks finished. She does not have much hope left for herself. We are in such a society filled with this kind of mindset. And for me to start my career in the film industry with no filmy background, no connections, no financial backup, pursuing my passion seemed highly impossible. For this, I would share more about my childhood journey to understand further the hardship I have faced. At school and college, I always used to look forward to events, not just to participate in extracurricular activities but to listen to the achievers who were invited as chief guests. Motivational speeches were something I always gave importance to while growing up. I used to keep CLARITY OF THOUGHT since the beginning.

My journey here will come in handy to some.

2
MAKEUP YOUR MIND GIRL!

After returning from the vacation, at an airport, as usual, few recognized me as an actor and came up to get pictures clicked. One of them had a baby girl and a toddler. She came up to me, and just as many approached and always asked and were curious to know how I maintain my daughter's hair as she has long, beautiful hair. And my response to all of them is, "If we want to, we always find a way to get it."

Also, she complimented me, saying I looked very young for my age. This joint statement made amongst women doesn't seem like a compliment.

And, yes, everybody is very surprised how I manage/do it without any nanny/help to keep me fit and always look presentable for my profession, where our appearance matters the most. Ironically, all dolling up has become part of my life, especially now. But once upon a time, it was taboo at my place as my father was strictly against girls giving importance to makeup. And he could have been more encouraging and refrained from my mother from giving any emphasis or prominence to beauty. However, by nature, my mother was simple and helpless in situations that did not matter to her much. For actors, makeup is like armor. It is a part of the world of the character we will be playing. It helps us remember the ways of the character, get into her skin, and embody it.

I believe makeup is sacred for an artist. We are bound to it like a painter is to their brush, or a dancer is to their music. The world's preoccupation with beauty often complicates our relationship with makeup as actors. The first time I came across the duality of beauty was when my father asked me not to wear makeup.

During my adolescence, I began my destined journey in the world, and my life as a performer and actor began to take shape during that phase. Incidentally, at this time, I also began to understand the world's ways. This new gush of life replaced my inability to understand my place in the world. A dilemma I encountered in my journey as a professional actor was my relationship with makeup.

I was only seven or eight and watched my aunt get dressed. We were getting ready for an event, probably because my mother never wore makeup and was a simple person who took joy in simple things. My aunt saw me gazing at her and called me towards her.

"Dear, come here. Would you like to try applying lipstick?" she asked me endearingly. I was scared. I didn't reply.

She pulled me towards her and dabbed lipstick on me in one smooth stroke. That was the first time I ever had some unnatural color on my face, yet it made me feel beautiful. It felt a little liberating, and it was fun. I was happy. I went to the hall where my dad was sitting.

When my dad saw me, something irked him and triggered a blind rage, and he reprimanded me for wearing makeup. I was terrified because I did not understand my mistake. My family soon interrupted him, suggesting that I was only a child and it did not matter. But his rage took a toll on me, and I broke down, angry at him for scolding me for wearing makeup. He disagreed with the principles of extravagance in life. So, after this incident, he always stopped me from wearing makeup.

As an actor, I would wear makeup before my performances and during shoots. Regardless, my father did not want me to wear lipstick and other makeup products at home or for personal events. I was puzzled by this change in attitude. It was alright for me to wear makeup at work, but I was supposed to embody the simplicity of a saint who does not like makeup at home. It made me think about how we initiate perceptions of material objects. For my father, makeup was an accessory in the life of an actor.

The connotations that it came with were unacceptable outside of a performance space. Even though I have always respected my father, I was upset by his reprimands. In retrospect, I understand his words were to protect me. His ways of reprimanding me were to ground and remind me of where I come from. I have always been a person who takes pleasure in celebrating a moment. The opportunities and resources that my parents provided me were at my disposal to benefit from. My father and mother came from a world of simplicity and struggle.

Like my mother, I enjoy simple things. I hardly dress up outside of my shooting days or showbiz events. I wear a beautiful dress that can augment my smile and pose for the camera. Today, when my daughter enters the room and watches me getting ready for an event, I take joy in knowing she is lucky enough to have all the freedom to express herself just how she wishes.

My upbringing was full of rules and regulations. My parents had several rules for my brother and me. We would wake up at four every morning, shower, perform our prayers, and start studying. It's funny how we would doze off during these early morning study sessions. Throughout the day, we are expected to perform sincerely in school, finish our homework on time, and not watch television. My father would put his hand on the television after coming home to check if it was hot. A hot surface would indicate that our television was on before he arrived home. Thus, because of his close check on all our activities, we would often refrain from breaking the rules of the house. I love my parents more than anything and will always remain indebted to them for all their sacrifices to raise me. As children, we hardly understand what goes through a parent's mind. Over the years, I have learned that parents pressure themselves, so no one says anything to their children. Sometimes, this pressure also falls upon the children, leading to communication gaps. However, I have learned that we can always overcome these pressures and unite as a family. I was never allowed to wear jeans, pants, or Western dresses. Thankfully, we had uniforms at school. However, I couldn't express my sense of dressing according to my will and wish in college. It wasn't a particularly flattering look. Our attire was just one thing that we decided for us girls. My father did not allow vanity. If I ever stood in front of a mirror for longer than 2 minutes, he would say,

"What does it matter how you look? What will come of it? Go study instead!"

He was probably right about this. However, as children, you do not often see their perspective. As a girl, my mind was occupied with something else. I was plagued by doubt regularly. Wasn't I capable of doing something on my own?

As a young girl, I suffered from my insecurities. I couldn't seem to persuade myself that I was beautiful! No one could tell me differently. No pals would brag about me and tell me how nice I looked. Today, my thoughts are different. For me, beauty comes from acceptance. You accept how you look. You acknowledge that your body will change because it is fighting to keep you alive, no matter what. You have to let your body do its thing! The key to looking beautiful is to truly accept yourself and be proud of what you have. You have to invest in yourself. When you look in the mirror, try not to hate the person who looks back at you. Once you resolve to accept yourself as you are, things will begin to change in your life. However, for me, this resolution took work.

I have a career where I must be conscious about my appearance. This is because I am working under the all-seeing camera. Any little "flaw" will stay recorded for life, and it's for the world to see. As actresses, women are more prone to judgments and criticism than expected. We are public figures, after all. We are putting ourselves out there, and it is hard to explain How scary that is. However, my journey as an actress changed the way I perceived myself. It has been a very uplifting experience for me.

During my TV acting days, I was not all that good-looking to play a lead role. I have played roles that were twice as old as my age. Some casting professionals rejected me for this reason. Naturally, this made me perceive my beauty very negatively. There were days when I felt discouraged and low. I have questioned my determination to become an actress. However, over time, I have understood that age is just a number. I have never paid heed to people and their comments about my appearance, and I won't let them either. A closer look at some of my favorite movies from around the world reveals that expressions and acting abilities are way more engaging than the appearance of an actor. With time, we can make movies where collaboration supersedes these superficial anxieties of our times. The arrival of Over-the-Top platforms has made stories from around the country and the world accessible to so many of us. I am convinced that in no time. Producers agree that our viewers are ready to watch stories for the content and how it is made rather than just for a few subjective desirable points.

Growing up, I watched very few movies. I was never keen on acting. However, certain movies did impact my perception. More than those typical hero-heroine-villain movies, I was, somehow, drawn to "content-oriented movies." The portrayal of strong female characters, showcasing not only beauty but grit as well, served to nourish my longing to watch meaningful movies. I always wondered if I was drawn to their looks, dialogue delivery, and acting skills or mesmerized by the whole idea of such films. As time passed, I could craft a unique filmmaking palette for my interests. Although entering the film industry was never on my to-do list, I was sure of what I did not wish to do in an acting career. Today, if I had to name a film that affected me the most, I would fail miserably in calling one. I have watched over ten thousand movies, and there is no shortage of good films in the cinema. One of my fondest memories takes me back to the day I first watched Charulata. Satyajit Ray's portrayal of female characters somehow carries a unique blend of power, repressed passions, and emotional turmoil amid political upheaval. Beautiful, mesmerizing, and sumptuous all the way through, Charulata made me think about the most polished and sophisticated form of filmmaking. My young mind was inundated by this alluring and arresting depiction of love, loyalty, and yearning seen through the eyes of a lonely housewife. Every character in the movie walked on a different stage of life while accurately depicting the upper-class lifestyle of 19th century India. Even though the theme resonated more with a faraway land, it caressed my mind with a new touch. I could feel the emotional dilemma of a woman even though those one-liners, for the idea was to portray a strong character without being verbose.

Films are the most influential media in society, and in this industry, for commercial purposes, where it predominantly depends on the factors that can sell the film/or drive the audience to come to the theatres rather than focusing on what needs to be done.

In college, I was enacting in a play and backstage while getting ready. While applying a skin foundation, one of the makeup artists commented, "Aaiyyo, your skin is so rough, like a boy's skin. Why don't you take care of your skin?"

He asked in a loud voice, and I felt very embarrassed. I didn't know what to say, so I kept quiet. He just laughed and finished applying makeup.

I have seen, heard, and experienced such comments about my looks and appearance. Still, I have learned from them all that being comfortable in your skin, completely accepting yourself, and respecting yourself is highly imperative in life.

3
STORYBOOK

"Amma, can you tell me a monster story?" my cute little one asked me.

"Oh! My brave daughter, why is there always a monster story? Instead, shall I read a hare and a rabbit story to you?!!"

"Ok, mommy," God, I cuddled her, gave her hundreds of kisses, hugged her while lying on the bed, and started reading a story before she nodded off.

I love reading bedtime stories to my child. I am grateful to know my daughter enjoys them and does a lot of reading independently. She loves reading so much that she says she prefers books over candies! Knowing that she likes to read books and see the world intimately brings me great joy. Reading books can make you a sympathetic person willing to understand more than one perspective on life. One such day, I was helping my daughter pick another book at the bookstore. A stranger saw us, recognized me, approached me to appreciate my work, and talked to my daughter. They found her adorable and spoke warmly to her. They shared their blessings for a better future for my daughter and left. However, my daughter had several questions for me after they left. The stranger did not fit any binaries of man and woman, and they were unique in appearance and expression.

I never get annoyed with her questions and try to answer them patiently. On this day, I was happy to answer her and tell her about transgender people. My daughter's questions reminded me of my childhood curiosity. I always had a lot of questions about the world. Like every child, I held on to "why" and "what" to learn as much as possible about the world. However, my parents were different in their expressions of love. My questions would often need to be addressed in the hum-drum of life. Building our home and ensuring our stomachs were full was a priority for them. They did not have the time to encourage my cerebral musings.

Parents are encouraged to be vigilant and conscious of their child's needs. Moreover, giving your child a healthy amount of space and time is essential for their overall well-being. I aspire to be there for all my child's questions and needs. At the same time, I will also give her the space to cultivate her own choices and act upon them.

As parents, much of our time goes into deciding how to negotiate a child's autonomy. We want to give them all the freedom in the world, but sometimes, unconsciously, we impose our needs and wants onto our children. My father had great aspirations for me, which entailed reading complicated philosophical texts and embracing an intellectual life. I, on the other hand, was a lost bee. I would escape life through my daydreams and fantasies, too caught up in my world of fancy and imagination to pay attention to the intellectual demands of the people around me. However, I also wanted my parents to be thoughtful about other things – I would wish them to decorate the house a certain way or communicate more freely. However, the times differed, and articulation was not our greatest weapon.

Now, I am a mother and struggle to meet all the expectations of my child, family, and society. I understand better than ever what drove my parents to make their decisions. Parents always want the best for their children. They pray and wish for their child's safety and well-being at all hours of the day and night. They chastise, love, beat, and even console us. Parents use several strategies to help their children. Some people follow the policy of being extremely courteous, while others are more rigorous. Though parents should not be overly strict, it is equally valid that a lack of discipline can harm a child. Hence, effective communication and mutually respectful relationships are vital. Even if they don't want to, parents must sometimes be strict. They chastised us so that we may learn from our mistakes and avoid repeating them in the future. In addition, parents frequently criticize their children when they perform poorly in exams. Parents work hard to ensure that their children understand every subject. When a youngster does badly in exams, parents express their fury without much thought to older generations. Sometimes, our parents are overly concerned about our safety. They fear that we will be in danger, so they become harsh and restrict us from doing certain activities or going somewhere. But we must remember that even while they reprimand and punish us, they love us equally with passion and concern.

"You are totally responsible for yourself, whatever you do! It is no good to blame the environment and heritage. My mother and father were like this; therefore, I am like that." —J Krishnamurti.

My father's concern took the form of reprimanding me for liking storybooks and comic books. I was young and found the fantasy world of comic book action and fiction very engaging. However, my father believed reading prominent writers and understanding their teachings was important.

Today, in the world of cinema, I meet veteran actors and hear them namedropping names of thinkers, philosophers, and creators. I also remember my father's scolding. However, this does not mean his approach is the only way of life. I built my world of acting and creativity with the help of my imagination. Art's role is to awaken and heal us. Art can belong in myriad shapes and stories; we must find what soothes us. We cannot blame others for the outcomes of our life. Yes, we can acknowledge the role of other people in our lives.

However, adulthood is about figuring out what troubles us and finding solutions to sustain us. My brother and I always knew that our story differed from other families. Our parents did not make the same choices as other parents – these decisions could be financial or social. At first, we were a lower-middle-class family. We lived as tenants and would often relocate. However, things started getting better with my family's determination. Moreover, my father was a solemn person who made sure there were savings for us to rely on. We were raised to avoid becoming spendthrifts and ensure we only had as much as we needed. I recall going to the grocery store with my mother – it would be like a vacation! I would enjoy watching her add items to the basket. However, I was never allowed to buy sweets or chocolates – no matter how much I liked them.

As a dreamy kid, this restriction would make me daydream about rivers of chocolate and me diving right into it! I wanted to swim in a river made of chocolate. In contrast, my family believed having chocolate once a month could also be dangerous to our health. It was a case of extremes, festered by each other's stubbornness. My desire for chocolate was minor compared to my father's desire to ensure our bright and faultless future. Like most in our country, my mother would play the buffer and hide tiny amounts of money so she could get a sweet treat now and then. So much of my gentleness I owe to her generosity, so much of my ability to withstand any peril, I owe to my father's strict guidance. Things took a sharp turn when I switched to a new and modern school after my primary education. We shifted to a new locality and climbed the ladder of social prosperity like other middle-class people.

I encountered many non-Kannada-speaking children who came from relatively more affluent families. So many of them grew up with their extended family near them. I began to drift from my peers and grew conscious of our differences. The school was Christian, and the teachers were determined to ensure that all students had holistic development. Extracurricular activities were as important as studies, to the extent that teachers would call parents to discuss the latest results in the child.

My dad grew up without parents; hence, he was not in touch with many people in his family. He had a massive group of intellectually rigorous friends. I was young and conscious of my intellectual ineptitude in front of them. They came from prominent families and received a very elite education. In place of these troubles, I recall an incident where I participated in a play. My parents were eager to watch me participate in extracurricular activities and would have several conversations with my teachers. Once, I became a part of a special event. I was to participate in a scene depicting the birth of Jesus Christ, and I was asked to wear a white dress for the Christmas event. I did not have one, and my father dismissed any request to purchase one. I felt extremely conflicted.

On the one hand, the teachers expected me to give my best in all my activities. On the other hand, my father could not purchase this essential item for the performance. I was taken aback by what was happening and cried a lot when I could not get the dress for my play. The morning before leaving for the function, my father found a shop open at 7 am in the city and purchased a cheap white colored dress. My teachers were dissatisfied with the presentation and had to change my character at the last minute. This minor incident has taught me such a big lesson in parenting. The pressure parents have to be under! The world is an unfair place. What becomes of us is highly dependent on the resources that are available to us. Hence, parents become burdened with the thought of not doing enough for their children – when they already provide more than they could have. When I look back, I do not think anyone was at fault. Not my teacher for requesting a particular dress, not me for participating in the event, and not my father for being unable to purchase the dress.

Circumstances can change the way we deal with our day-to-day hurdles. Parenting has always been a difficult job for which no one prepares you. You may find solace in the idea that, while prior generations did not suffer the same issues that we do, parenting was not always easy. Any parent will agree that the difficulties are all worthwhile in the end! A crammed daily schedule is the price of modernization. Most parents have little time for relaxation, recreation, or even sleep during the day. Not only that, but both mothers and fathers are balancing jobs, housework, and, of course, parenting. Additional social pressures such as gatherings, parties, birthdays, and caring for aging parents must be noticed. Spending time together doing "nothing" was considered normal and beneficial a generation ago, but it is now deemed unproductive. All family members are expected to make good use of their time by participating in some activity or another!

Furthermore, children are nurtured urgently to achieve goals and not squander time. Expecting them to thrive in everything, from academics to sports and hobbies, can be stressful. School, schoolwork, extracurricular activities, and devices can all overstimulate your children, leaving them physically and emotionally exhausted. With so much pressure to perform at a young age, it's understandable that some children believe, "I am not good enough." It isn't uncommon for parents and children to feel overwhelmed and overworked in the face of such circumstances.

I was a disciplined child of strict parents who did not let us watch much television. My father had a job where he was his boss – he could come home any time of the day to check on us and make sure we were studying and spending our time wisely. Because the older TVs would get hot after being switched on, the first thing my father did after entering the house was to check if the TV was hot! If it was hot, it meant we were watching television and not studying as we ought to. My brother and I feared our fathers' wrath and would often figure out ways to evade his cross-questioning and steal some time in front of the television. Like everyone else in the country, we were obsessed with television. We enjoyed watching all sorts of cartoons, serials, and movies that were aired on television. It was a delightful escape from the monotony of our lives. Especially for a shy child like me, it was a reminder that if I let go of my fears, I could perform and express myself as delightfully as the people on the screen did.

We sustained ourselves on an adventurous televisual diet of stories from the Jungle Book, Ramayana, Mahabharata, and Disney. Through their stories of war and friendship, we learned of the world from our little living room. The irony of not being allowed to watch television always baffled me. My father was a theatre practitioner. Furthermore, he was delighted with my theatre performances as well. I was encouraged to do extracurricular activities, especially theatre and drama. Then why could I not watch television? In his eyes, the theatre was an enlightening experience that could teach us life lessons and help us evolve as good performers. My father was quick to discern the harmful effects of overconsumption of television. He ensured we formed our minds before fading into the bliss of television's non-stop entertainment. Earlier, I was puzzled and anxious because of his reprimands. Still, growing up, I realized there was a lesson in his warnings.

Despite being from the world of theatre, I was not in love with acting as a child, and it was a mere compulsion of my father that I was part of theatre plays. In 10th grade, I attended the tuition classes just like all my peers. My teacher would address me as "Nayika" (translates to heroine) because he had seen me perform and liked my acting. Hence, because of the way people acknowledged my acting, I was aware of my skill but not ready to embrace it entirely. I was highly introverted and felt the acting world was daunting because actors are expected to be inhibited. As an artist, I was still discovering the limits of being, so praise and accolades were initially scary. The added burden of not having any inhibitions was a big obstacle at the beginning of my career. I participated in the critically acclaimed theatre workshop (Benaka Makkala Nataka tanda) in Bengaluru during my schooling years. I attended the workshop three years ago and was initially quite underwhelmed by the experience. I joined these workshops because my parents believed they were necessary for my children's personality development.

During my performance in a workshop, my father's friend (Mr. TN Seetharam, a renowned personality) saw me perform. This performance was also the first time I was facing the camera, all of 14 years of age. I was about to join class 8, and the performance included 60 other kids. However, my performance won accolades, and I was selected for a role on the television screen. The play I was performing for was showcased on Doordarshan. I was on screen for multiple teleplays and telefilms during my schooling years, which helped me grow and develop as an artist.

In her book "The Conscious Parent," Shefali Tsabary states that you will only accept your child to the extent that you accept yourself. While this may appear to be an easy task, the truth is that most of us do not practice self-acceptance and self-love. In a world filled with continual comparisons and peer pressure, we must accept ourselves and educate our children to accept themselves. Acceptance is the key to creating free thinkers and happy children. Parents can tell themselves, "I understand that I am a human being before I am a parent." When there is an accepted culture in the family, regardless of external influences, the core of your and your child's existence remains stable and undisturbed. When raising children, one of the parents' most common mistakes is allowing society's standards to precede their inner parenting voice. At the start of one's parenting adventure, one may feel befuddled. However, when your bond with your child grows more substantial, you will discover that you know your child better.

There may come a time when you feel your feet moving backward. Like me, you may find yourself retracing the movement of your life in an attempt to understand your decisions. Well, I have accepted the calming swings of the pendulum. We must embrace the highs as well as the lows of our life. Most importantly, we keep moving, evolving, and elevating to the tune of life. A parent plays a critical role in our lives. They are the bearers of our social well-being in the early days of our life. I was aware that my parents were very different from other parents. Their story was unique, a sum of the experiences they had endured in their lives. However, that had its impact on our lives.

If you understand this early in life, your battle is half won already; yes, take responsibility for your consequences and refrain from playing a blame game.

4

ALARM

"Ta, Thai Thai Tat... Aa Thai Thai Tat" « - I watched my daughter start her dance classes; it was the first day she got introduced to dance. I was surprised to see that she was really enjoying herself and focused on following the instructions given by her Guru. This reminded me of my childhood when my mother used to sneak me out of the house to take Bharatanatyam classes without my father's knowledge, as he never wanted to encourage me to pursue dance as my passion. I was upset, and when I asked him the reason - his excuse was, "What if you spent all these years learning dance, and when you are ready to get married, if your to-be husband refrains you from dancing, all your dedicating and hard work will go in vain". Still, ironically, I'm married to a dance family.

The moral of the story is that no matter what, children are influenced by their parents, who try to shift their paradigms to accept that girls will have to obey their parents' views or their husbands' choices without leaving any choice for themselves. Dance is, was, and will always be my dominant passion. I strongly felt from my gut that I was a gifted dancer; alas, I couldn't pursue it. My mother tried to help me not to give up my dreams; similarly, I want my daughter to pursue her passion no matter what she is inclined to because I feel that life is empty without any passion).

I have immense gratitude for my mother for instilling faith in me and reassuring me to hold on to the faith, most importantly, having tremendous patience to wait for that day- to embrace it. My father directs stage plays; however, I have never had an opportunity to act in his direction, not even once. I remember very well that my brother and I would accompany our parents for stage rehearsals after school hours when I was a kid. My mother used to be associated in whichever way – designing costumes, handling logistics, and caring for the artiste. For one instance, my mother had enacted one of the plays under my father's direction. I recall that my short-tempered father started yelling at my mother for not adhering to the instructions while enacting her role. Those days, I was highly tense and worried for my mother until her performance was completed.

As I write this, I realize that even though I talk a lot about my childhood, I seldom talk about my mother. As did mine, both parents are very influential in any child's life. Yet I have significantly less to talk about my mother, probably because my father was the doer in our family and my mother was a healer. In my family, the gender roles were stringent.

Everyone has their weight to pull to do, but does a relationship work like that? Especially if that relationship is marriage. When I look at my mother, especially since she is now older and does not keep well much, it was that one incident when my mother was suffering a lot from an umbilical hernia (when part of your intestine bulges through the opening in your abdominal muscles near your belly button). This time would be her third time receiving the same surgery; my mother is a person who bears any pain no matter what, but this time, the pain was excruciating. She couldn't help but burst into tears. I can never forget the phone ringing in the middle of the night when my father called me; his shaky voice asked us to come over. My husband and I rushed to my parent's house, only to find my mother lying on her bed crying because of the excruciating pain. We decided not to waste any more time and took her to the hospital.

The doctors at the hospital informed us that our mother's condition was serious because this was the 3rd time something like this had happened, and she should be admitted immediately. We agreed; we had never seen my mother go through something like this before. She kept trembling after consuming several painkillers because of the excruciating pain. My mother is one of those women who admits and understands that pain is inevitable for a woman; hence, she prefers to keep her sufferings to herself. She never complained about anything; all she ever wanted to do was to be a good mother and wife, so her number one aim was to keep us happy; she would suppress her feelings deep down, probably burying them in her stomach.

Now that I think of it, my mother holding her woes and pains to herself in her belly can symbolize the abdominal pain she was experiencing because of the hernia. I was terrified because the person who never complained was in tears. This had to happen someday. I knew it. I have always argued with her to prioritize her health, but she never listened. My brother decided to stay the night at the hospital with my mother. Even at that stage, in that terrible pain, my mother whispered and told me to take care of the milkman and the maid. She could not let go of her duties or forget about her role in the family. At that moment, I told my mother to relax and that I would take care of it, but when I think about it, even in that condition, all my mother could think about was her household and the things she needed to take care of. She did not think about herself at all!

Until a few years ago, this was the norm that a woman would only think about her household and nothing else. In those school days, during festivals, my father was particular about my brother, and I woke up early, around 4:30 am or 5:00 am. Even today, I feel like an organic alarm rings in my mind, asking me to wake up and get studying! We were strictly told to shower first and could only participate in festivities. Of course, I don't have any complaints about it now, but then, something always felt peculiar to me. After we finished getting ready, my father would ask me to help my mother in the kitchen, but he had yet to ask my brother the same. I had to do all the house chores, like cooking, cleaning, sweeping, grinding chutney on a stone grinder, serving food, etc. Even though I do not mind doing the chores, I like doing these things. But then I always had this question as to why my brother didn't have to do so. I expected to do these chores because this was expected of a girl. After she is born, an Indian parent thinks of marriage first, so she is reared to be good at chores rather than other things.

A girl was meant to care for her family; whatever she did was for her family's sake. After the surgery, we offered to help with the hospital bills, but my father is very righteous; he does not accept money from his children. My mother started to worry about the hospital fees and money spent on her treatments even though we were financially doing well now. My father was very active in theatre and deeply passionate about it. He had also established a Kannada monthly theatre magazine, "EE Masa Nataka," a highly circulated and well-reputed magazine amongst the theatre intellectuals. It had more than 5,000 subscribers across the globe, and overseas theatre lovers, too, had subscribed.

We had to do all the posting details for the theatre magazine every month, like pasting the addresses and stamps to each magazine by hand and giving it to the nearby post office. For that, my mother was assigned to cut the individual postal address from the lengthy sheet and paste it into every magazine. It was a very tedious task and took long hours to complete. My brother and I used to give a hand as we could not see the plight of my mother working additional hours after completing the household chores/other domestic work. This continued even though my mother had carried pain in her stomach because of a hernia and post-surgery, which was highly unbearable and shocking. I have had many confrontations with my father about this topic, but in vain.

Even though my parents were like that, it's not like they were fighting or disrespecting each other; they were very clear about their roles in the family and were okay with it. This wasn't just about my mother but most women I had seen and been close to as I grew up. I always wondered, since my childhood, why women could not be financially independent. Still, a couple of my aunts were earning. Yet they chose to give their salaries to their husbands every month. Hence, even if you were a homemaker or a working woman, you were still not financially independent.

I ended up discussing this issue with my mother when I was younger, asking why she was not financially independent, to which she replied, saying that she did have a job back in the day. Still, she sacrificed it to care for the kids, the kitchen, and the house, which was her role in the household. The money matter was my father's responsibility; he would take care of it because it was part of our culture and tradition. When I heard this, I didn't question this philosophy. Still, I embraced it instead, thinking that this was probably how the world worked and that I, too, would have to face the same gendered roles when I grew up and married. This notion of not sharing responsibilities is precisely why this whole thing is alarming. This was the norm. Even movies, songs, and media back in the day broadcasted gendered roles this way, where the mother and the father had distinct roles.

This was how marriage was perceived back in the day; partners had roles to play in the family; the woman was meant to cook, clean, heal, and care for their family. In contrast, the men were told to manage the finances, maintain discipline, and handle deeds outside the house.

My family shifted houses a lot. After completing high school and moving to college, my father built a bigger house in a better area; he was a professional civil contractor. Now I realize how blessed I am to have my husband in my life, and we often discuss that one should not depend on others for emotional satisfaction because it is all about you and your mind. Times are changing, and so are definitions of social institutions of marriage because man has finally realized how to achieve any emotional and intellectual satisfaction. No one is perfect. Only loving yourself will provide the peace and happiness one is looking for. A partner is not needed for one's feelings to be fulfilled. What is love, then? Love is knowing and accepting who you are first and then others. When a person seeks validation and approval from their partner, that marriage is not working out. It has problems. Once you seek validation from your partner, they will take you for granted. One must understand that if you are reaching out to seek confirmation from your partner, the problem is you. You are not healed and have not accepted yourself for who you are. You cannot do the same for others unless you have healed yourself.

As a modern woman, I recognize that we do not have to depend on someone or a partner to be happy, peaceful, or loved. One must look within to quench the need to be acknowledged, validated, loved, relaxed, and joyful.

But then, what is marriage? Most people who are married in 21st-century Indian society are together because they are in the habit of being together, not because of love, and that is okay because every human being is different. They have different temperaments and moods, and most people deal with their issues, insecurities, etc. From my experience, from not only being married for so long but also from observing several other marriages, I learned that to have a loving marriage, when two people come together in pursuit of happiness and companionship, one must meet their partner halfway, intellectually, physically, and emotionally.

As defined, an ideal marriage is a social institution without rules. Marriage cannot be confined to boxes; it's a bond that two people create to support each other through life's journey, through thick and thin, treating each other equally.

True companionship includes - physical, emotional, financial, intellectual, and connectivity in a relationship. In a relationship, patience is the key; avoid jumping to conclusions and wait for it. Try to think when your mind is calm.

5
ROSES AND THORNS

It was a busy day, swamped with a couple of events to attend and an AD campaign to shoot. However, I ensured that I strictly maintained discipline in my routine and gave importance to my health/fitness, which was paramount for me as a mother. If you have children/kids who are school-going and their parents can relate to how busy it will be during the mornings – from waking up your kid to fixing breakfast, packing lunch for them, and finally rushing to board them to the school bus, they would need to multitask. I have signed up for a yoga instructor who comes to my place so that I don't miss aasana practice regularly, at least three times a week. I highly recommend this to everybody else. If you take care of your body, the body will automatically help you take care of your mind. We need the connection between the mind, body, and soul to be intact.

Just then, I finished my practice and came down from my studio on the upper floor of my house in a hurry to be surprised to see my daughter all set and ready to go to school on time, all done but not well by my dear husband. I must admit that when my husband tries his best to help me with household chores or gives a hand in kid's grooming, I love his effort even though it's double work for me later. *"Mommy, Dad has messed up trying to tie my hair, and my socks are not intact, Mommy...!! Do it properly, Mommy; if not, I'll start crying now..."*

Hahahaha…my baby is late for her school. She is a little fussy about certain things like she wants her hair to be tied in a particular way and her dress should match her wish; like most toddlers, they test our patience. And thank God for my patience and my husband's sense of humor. Trust me …which is an excellent help in such situations in a family. *"Come on, darling, I'll help fix things," I said, and things moved on smoothly."*

We are familiar with the adage, 'Behind every successful man, there is a woman.' But how many of us know that the opposite is true as well? Behind every successful woman is a man who is by her side—ever-loving, caring, compassionate, and most of all, supportive of her every action. It has been said that marriage is the union of two wandering souls waiting to meet their perfect match. Now, every marriage is not picture-perfect. The most common discrepancy in a marriage is that the husband is vastly more successful career-wise when compared to his wife.

I'm all for successful people and wish everyone a fruitful career. But how often do we see married women making their mark worldwide? That's a question we all need to think about.

The conversation around marriage reminds me of an incident that happened to me recently. My comeback movie is 'HOPE' (after having my baby). I was delighted to hear that it was streaming now on Amazon Prime – people worldwide could watch my work. Amidst the chaos, the most heart-warming moment for me was when I saw my husband jumping around in happiness. I was elated to see my life partner celebrate my success more than I did! He was happy for me, and I took pride in his happiness. I had tears in my eyess, and at once, I felt gratitude for his presence in my life for the past twenty years. Being married can be challenging. Sometimes, it's more like the icing chunk that gets stuck on your nose during the cake smash—good intentions, but awkward results! "Living happily ever after" takes a lot of work, so whether you've been married for years or getting married, marriage takes work! The other day, one of my relatives told me, *"Hey, I saw your movie recently; you have done a good job."* "Oh, *thank you. So, kind of you"! I said. "Honestly, you are lucky to have such an understanding husband,"* she said. Even though I have heard this no matter how many times, I still fail to understand why they say that. I just smiled at her and was petty about such a mentality. And, yes, I moved on as usual.

Marriages in India, like relationships between Indian married couples, have developed over time. There was a time when women had to give up their careers to care for their families. Trying to find the ideal companion is akin to expecting the unattainable. Marriage can be tricky since you must share many things in this relationship. The problem is neither marriage nor a man and a woman, husband and wife. You will experience similar issues in any position where you must share a lot with others. You usually have to share the same place, the same everything in a marriage or cohabitation.

I have known my husband for a long time; we married in the year 2005. Our story is straight out of a film! We are stronger together. Through the years, we have been there for each other through all our struggles. No one understands me better than he does, simply because of his loving presence in my life all these years. I am grateful because we have come to build a long, loving, healthy, and highly romantic relationship over the years. However, it is not all cake and cherries – we have also been through challenging ordeals. Our support for each other during the tough times strengthened my belief in our friendship and marriage.

Looking back at my past, I realize I was in a very dark phase before meeting him. As I have mentioned before, I lacked self-confidence and faith in myself. I was insecure because I had pre-existing belief systems that told me I was not good enough – whether for my appearance or how I lived my life.

When you do not feel comfortable in your skin, you cannot give back to the world. It seemed like the world, and I was dissonant – moreover, I could not participate in the world like I wanted to. I stopped myself from becoming a part of things and celebrating myself. Look at me now.

Nothing in my life is less than larger than life! I have realized love's tremendous potential; it can help you overcome several obstacles. Therefore, I should share the story of my marriage. If there is anyone in the world who feels caged in their current circumstances, scared of taking a step ahead in their lives, I hope my story finds you.

I was a budding TV actor, and my inhibitions began to overpower my life, pulling me down. I joined my college but continued to have crippling self-confidence issues. I was in my shell, unable to let go of my thoughts and fears to be able to participate in life. My father suggested I speak with my professor, Dr. Geetha Ramanujam. She was already an established name in the world of theatre. Despite my reserved nature, I decided to challenge myself and approach her. I met with her in our college staff room and conveyed my regards. She was interested in me after I shared my previous experiences in theatre and television and assigned me to a teleplay that would air on Doordarshan. It was a miracle that brought me to her, for I was so scared of the world that I could not have imagined finding the courage to carve my path. She was enigmatic, very well-educated, and a professor the world admired. She was strict, but everyone obeyed her willfully because of her powerful presence. It was an honor to be mentored by her in the early days of my career. I remember her describing me as a disciplined student when I first met her. It is a compliment that lights up my days even today. Everything about Dr. Geetha Ramanujam greatly influenced and inspired my life. She was also a significant reason to have learned and developed a deep interest in Women's Empowerment.

When I joined the team for the teleplay, I was made the protagonist of the play (Nijagallina Rani) in a team full of theatre veterans. I was excited to play the part, but my nervousness and fears overtook me. I was the cast's youngest member and initially found the pressure exhilarating. The play's lead characters were essayed by the renowned musician Sri. RK Padmanabh Mrs. Vidhya Murthy, a renowned TV and film actor, usually portrays important/supporting roles. (I address her as Amma because she has been a very kindhearted elderly friend, giving me guidance and help whenever I needed it.) However, I overcame my fears and performed the teleplay. Today, when I am harsh on myself and encounter obstacles that make me doubt myself, I remind myself that I can overcome anything with time and sincere effort. Every one of us develops a way to survive our childhood. Some of us are lucky and blessed to be in an environment where we do not have to defend ourselves or be self-absorbed and self-protect. Those who grew up like that grew up with open hearts. However, not all of us are that lucky. We grow up with so much pain, shame, and neglect. Because of that, we develop a habit of protecting ourselves and defending ourselves at all times, which shows up in our behavior.

During my college days, coincidentally, and though it was not my conscious decision, I started working for television as an artist. I was offered a lead role in a television soap when I finished college and married. I accepted the offer because of the financial instability. To my bad, the first three months of the shoot were held out of the city, very far away from my place. Each day, we had long hours of shoot (14 to 16 appx), so we had to board in a remote village with zero facilities, and it was a nightmarish experience for three long months. This traumatic experience left a terrible spot in my mind. As an artist, such an experience will make me less self-worth! Likewise, many incidents were encountered while I was part of television soaps, which shattered my self-confidence.

Now, let me tell my love–marriage story and how it all started. I was shooting for a teleplay, donning the role of a housemaid. I remember we were shooting in a big house for the film. I was the story's protagonist, working alongside some of the biggest names in the acting world. My colleagues were veteran actors from the theatre world, and I was just a young girl studying in my second year of college.

Moreover, I needed help to accustom myself to television and acting. The teleplay was important; it was to be aired on Doordarshan, and several important dignitaries were attached to it. I felt the pressure suffocate me, and one day, my cab was late to pick me up for the shoot, and I was reprimanded on set. This incident was a massive blow as someone struggling to associate myself with the acting world. I found a corner away from everyone and had a breakdown. I felt lost and was beginning to lose faith in myself.

However, in the darkness, there was a silver lining. Additionally, my silvery lining looked prince charming from the world of joy. A young man appeared and smiled at me; he extended his hand to shake hands, "Hi, am Amith Srivatsav, naam toh suna hoga, ha ha ha ha," … and my hero stood before me there in a very Hindi filmy style. Instantly, I felt better than I did before. He was good to me and supported me throughout the shoot. He made me laugh and settled my nerves effortlessly. This new individual in my life was also a college-going guy, and I was attracted to him. Bless my fortune because he was attracted to me as well! Soon, we confessed our joy in finding each other, and he became one of the most influential people in my life — of course, he is my husband!

All love stories are a good mixture of roses and thorns, and so are ours. Despite our unconditional love for each other, we had to deal with society. We had similar preferences due to our age and social values. However, we came from distinct backgrounds and were answerable to our families for our choices. Moreover, we were very young. It was challenging to discern the magnitude of our situation. We wanted to study, build our respective careers, and keep our families. However, it felt like the world was crushing us. All our decisions became obstacles, and his parents disapproved and did not want to interact with me at first.

Furthermore, my husband's family asked him to make the ultimate choice. It had to be them or me. I cannot fathom my husband's feelings at that time. I am beyond grateful for what he did. I respected him all the more because he decided to choose me. After all, I was an essential part of his life. He wanted to tell his parents he would not bow down under pressure. Most importantly, my partner clarified that disregarding me was equivalent to ignoring his wishes. My partner came to my house with his belongings and love, and my father supported him in his endeavors.

Things moved on, and we settled into our lives. I had finished my mass communication course and secured a lecturer's position at a girls' college. My family was satisfied and felt I was beginning to stand firm on my feet. Meanwhile, my husband also started working at a company, and we began to build our lives. Eventually, we had a wedding where both our families were present. Many people from my husband's family shared my father's interests in theatre and literature and were overjoyed at our union.

However, we could feel that my husband's parents were yet to open up to us. Regardless, I was myself and did not let anyone's opinions pull me down.

Although explaining and implementing marriage customs has been difficult, there has been widespread agreement across cultures on one fundamental topic. Men should be the head of the family or the family's powerhouse. And the women should be the family's obedient party. However, with time, this idea has become obsolete. Today, I am a working professional and a mother. I often believe I have Goddess Durga's blessings and wisdom in me – I have had a rebellious streak throughout my life. If I live with an open heart and mind, the world will mend its ways and embrace me. However, I do feel demotivated when I think about how difficult it can be for women to negotiate with everyone's expectations. Like all women, I hope there comes a time when social responsibilities become easier for us all. However, knowing my husband is by my side and will support me has made everything worthwhile. He entered my life when these duties did not bind me, and yet, because of our commitment to each other, we have evolved with time and embraced these new roles. As my partner, he too grew into the role of a father, and together, we have been traversing through life's journey. Maintaining this balance is all the more difficult because I am an actress. I am incredibly grateful for the opportunities that come my way and for the love of my family and friends. However, like me, they are figuring out the right ways to enable a fruitful balance. Through communication and respect for each other, this balance can be customized per the needs of our profession and values.

Furthermore, we insist on staying in our comfort zones. This means we wish everyone would agree to our way of life. Sometimes, we find ourselves in tremendous pain because things do not work out the way we want them to. Being in a healthy marriage is a lesson in partnership. It allows us to find a middle ground where we can agree to disagree on matters and yet be kind to each other. When we build a safe place for equal communication and establish our love for each other foremost, it is easy to walk through the troublesome dilemmas of life. While a husband or wife may like to believe that everything is done out of love and for love alone, the fact remains that love only survives if it is cultivated. For two individuals to live successfully as husband and wife, they must understand each other in a way only true partners can. They must identify each other's needs and be willing to cooperate to satisfy them. I am grateful to have my husband by my side and to share the joys and burdens of being a mother. It could be a sweet joke he cracks at the end of a tiring day or his mini celebration of all my small and big successes.

It empowers me to continue my journey. As I continued reflecting on my past, I was reminded of when I decided to leave my perfect job. Having no financial support for both of us, no secure jobs, he was juggling between part-time jobs; I had just completed my master's and was fortunate enough to have found myself some respectful job; television was side my side hustle still then, that is when I decided to quit every job, I had to chase my dream, to become a 'FILM HEROINE' to be precise. Everyone was shocked to hear about my decision to quit working as a part-time lecturer. I decided I wanted to act in movies. The newfound joy I had found in expressing myself was telling me to challenge myself. Everyone thought I was out of my wits to make such a decision.

Making that decision was itself a big one for me. It was challenging. I knew I'd have to face a lot of consequences. That night, I had a conversation with my husband: *"Oh, don't worry, we have had so many discussions on this topic. We'll face it together."* He said. *"But how, will I tell this to Appa and Amma, do I give the resignation letter to our HOD at college? What if I don't make it? How will I tell the tele serial director that I won't be continuing the TV soap, as I want to become a film heroine? Oh god!! I can't sleep tonight?"* I was petrified. *"Everybody will shame me, laugh at me, they will feel sad for you, your parents will taunt you for marrying me!!"* I was in tears. *"Do you remember before our wedding, in your play, on the stage while you were presenting your monologue, I was stunned; I felt you should be working in movies; I told you that you deserve to be a movie star,"* he reminded me. Yes, it was my husband who taught me how to believe in myself and how to know my worth. After that day, we both faced nightmares for over five or six years. But that passion, that fires to get myself what I deserve, kept me going.

Throughout my life, I have relished such moments of clarity, where amidst the chaos, my heart and mind have come together to guide me and steer me from my path to more significant goals. Keeping your mind and body active all day and balancing is a must for anybody looking less hassle-free.

6

UMBRELLA

Recently, a wealthy family approached me for a wedding in their family. I had heard that actors and actresses are paid to attend weddings, but I was surprised to see such an offer come my way. I pondered this offer and wondered the ideal way to deal with it. I realized getting paid to attend someone's special day differed from my cup of tea. However, in my heart, I wished to meet and congratulate the happy couple regardless of the nature of their invitation. I met the couple and was glad to know the bride was a working professional like me. Through our interactions, we shared a similar approach to life, where our career and family would go hand in hand and not against each other. I congratulated her and shared my blessings with the happy couple. I wished for them to share a successful bond and be companions for life.

Attending a young professional woman's wedding reminded me of all those struggling days when I was newly married. I was eight or nine months into my marriage with my husband, and I was working as a UGC Project fellow under a HOD of Journalism subject at a girls' college. I was beginning to realize that acting played a far more significant role in my life than I was previously aware of. I was already working in television, but my heart was looking for more. I wanted to collaborate with other filmmakers and become a part of many more stories – augment their work with my acting skills. Given their upbringing, watching me leave behind a good job and struggle in cinema was incomprehensible to them, moreover, as an outsider in the film industry.

I had heard a lot about the industry being associated with a world of vulgarity and excess, and I was very different from my humble beginnings. I began to face the brunt of people's perceptions during social events and family functions. Sometimes, people would avoid approaching me or would meet and shower me with peculiar questions. "You are married now. Why not think about starting a family?" "Why did you quit your job as a lecturer?" "Why don't you work in television anymore?" I was petrified of such questions but decided to tackle my life one step at a time.

Looking back, I realize this was a very tough time for me. As a television actor, I would watch my male counterparts receive offers for film projects. Collaboration was a way of life in their world, and I felt like a bystander. I wondered when such a project would come my way, and I would finally break through the glass ceiling. I remember when a television director mocked my questions about upcoming film projects. I had faith in my craft and knew that with a suitable project, I could draw audiences to cinema halls. However, becoming a film actress comes with several other adages. It was problematic for my collaborators that I was married and had a history of performing for television. Like every other community in the world, cinema had its hierarchy. I realized I was considered a disadvantageous prospect in the beginning. With time, I received a few supporting roles, but I had an undying quench to become a leading film actress and mark my presence.

I remember once I was on a set shooting for a TV soap. I was waiting, sitting outdoors in the studio, as we were not privileged to have a caravan facility. A famous film actress had arrived on set, and everyone in the crew wanted to be the first to catch a glimpse of her. Film actors tend to carry a halo wherever they go. If I were to be honest, actors are quick to feel the absence of attention. Unlike other times, I felt a strong sense of loneliness. I realized there is no reason to underestimate myself and that I have all the qualities and talents demanded in films as a lead protagonist. We limit ourselves in our minds. I had to make a firm decision to quit working for television and start chasing my dream of being in films. Of course, I was well aware of my "drawbacks" – not only was I a married and television actress, but I also did not have a Godfather from the industry. After deciding to get into movies, the journey and the question of "what happens next?" preoccupied my mind. Most importantly, I had no film background and no person from my family to help me with anybody who belonged to the commercial film industry. I was worried that there was a signboard ahead of me that said 'impossible,' trying to stop me from achieving my dreams. The stress was even more evident because we were financially unstable. At the time, life took a physical and emotional toll on me. My husband and I were alone, struggling to make ends meet. My mother, being her kind soul, was by my side but faced the wrath of the people around us.

Furthermore, my husband had to make sacrifices and decided to change his plans. Previously, he aspired to study abroad, but given our circumstances, after his family disapproved of our relationship, he gave up his dreams and started working. Our financial burdens seemed to have no end – all our earnings were spent on repaying debts and loans. It seemed like a dark could always hover above us, preventing any ray of sunshine from blessing us and brightening our lives. In the middle of this chaos, an unfortunate incident rattled me.

During my first year of marriage, my husband fell down the stairs. He broke his colonic collarbone one day before Ganesh Chaturthi. It was unfortunate, and this accident put us all in shock. We rushed to the hospital, and after a doctor investigated his case, it was revealed that he would need major surgery to recover from the fall. Furthermore, I was also worried about arranging the finances for his healthcare. Apart from my father, I did not have many options to seek help from during this distress. It was a challenging situation. My husband was born on the day of Ganesh Chaturthi, so this accident seemed like a strange cosmic event.

I was in the early stages of my career, and his job was also reasonably new. By hook and crook, I arranged the money for his treatment and prayed for his successful recovery. The doctor informed me that under anesthesia, patients utter the names of their loved ones; usually, it is their mother. My husband kept calling me and wanted me to be beside him. Unfortunately, I had to work when he was in surgery. I tried to talk to my superiors and get some time off to see him but was dismissed. It was disheartening, but I am grateful he is by my side today. Even though our financial situation was dull, we knew we would do anything for each other. We had to face many challenges like this – I can't express all the pain we have gone through together. Much of our companionship was about my dreams and bringing them to life. We learned the lesson of independence and security. When the walls come crashing, one must always have the tools to fight the storm.

During this troublesome time, I began to feel demotivated. I felt like I was burdening my partner and my family with the weight of my dreams. Years went by, and I waited for a good opportunity that could cement my place in the world of movies. I was already in my late 20s; by now, I did not have children or a well-established movie career. However, I got a few supporting role opportunities. I thought about the sacrifices I had made to make films and how long it took for the dream to come true. I wanted to do quality roles that I would feel proud of doing.

Today, we appear to be role models for others because of the struggles we have fought against. But looking back, I am shocked to see I could fight these battles when I had so little faith in myself.

"Do the best you can until you know better. Then when you know better, do better." —Maya Angelou.

During the days when I approached directors and filmmakers for an opportunity, a common trend among familiar faces was to engage in idle chatter and spread rumors. As they say, the world is small, and we often find out who's saying what. I learned from a close friend that an individual who claims to be an intellectual TV and Film actress and is supposed to embody compassion and maturity was gossiping about me. Unbeknownst to her, she shared this with one of my good friends. My friend was deeply hurt upon hearing this, and she confronted the actress by asking, "Is Shwetha planning to leave her husband?" "No, why do you ask?" my friend replied. "Well, she's trying to get into movies. I thought she would ruin her family life," said the so-called intellectual and mature actress. That incident profoundly affected my friend, and when I learned about it, I was equally hurt. Why do people behave this way? What have I done to deserve this? I have never spoken ill of any woman or person in general, and my respect for such individuals plummeted immediately.

Yeah, after all the weight and emotional and mental exhaustion, I needed to continue to have faith in my craft. And look forward. I will someday watch myself on the big screen as a lead protagonist. It is easy to reflect on the past when I know what the future has in store for me. Waiting for our hard work to pay off is often one of the most complex career-building parts. I was at home, struggling to find good movie projects for many years together. My friends and family were concerned about my future, especially my father. He would try to convince me to look for alternatives because we needed more contacts in the industry.

Furthermore, my father was also concerned about my family's future. He wanted to ensure I was on the right path. In the middle of my chaotic life, he asked me to conduct a theatre workshop for kids. I felt ambushed by his request. Given my time working on television, I am an established actor. He insisted I build a theatre workshop for Government school kids – all from scratch and all by myself. I tried to explain my perspective to my father, but he insisted this was the next best step in my career. I was distraught, and the future was also looking bleak financially. I decided to take the opportunity and would travel to the venue with the help of public transport. Moreover, because of my past experiences and genuine respect for theatre, I built an intense workshop that the school's students enjoyed. However, it is said that the harder you work, the luckier you get. Amidst the cacophony of my theatre workshop, my father's disciple from a theatre background connected me with a filmmaker interested in associating with me on a low-budget movie production where I would essay the role of a negative character. Initially, I was apprehensive about the showrunners. I needed to figure out if the role was the best fit for me. However, I did not want to let go of an opportunity that had come my way after a long time. I asked my mother to wait for the forty-day film schedule. We were shooting far from Bengaluru. The film production offered no assistance to me – I had no makeup artists, costume designers, assistants, or any other help. Furthermore, we were asked to travel overnight in uncomfortable chair cars, our accommodation was significantly compromised, and we had to make do in abysmal conditions.

However, I sincerely enjoyed the filmmaking process regardless of the working conditions. I could sense that the creators were not very sure of what they wanted in the film, and hence, there would be quite a few inconsistencies. I believe such is the process of making a film – and one must enjoy it profoundly and cherish it to make a good film. Despite the highly technical nature of our work, I would always be surrounded by naysayers who wanted to know why I was working in the film industry despite being married. This reminds me of the time when I picked up another film. It was also a small production; however, this time, I had a few veteran actors in supporting roles by my side. Furthermore, the director was a television director who had worked with me before. The protagonist and the director were very keen to know why I was working in films after a successful stint in television and after getting married. However, they should have taken my outdoor requirements more seriously. I had no assistants to ensure I had umbrellas during our outdoor schedule. As a result, my entire skin was burnt, and the makeup refused to sit on my face for other parts of the schedule. Disparity during working hours can have long-term consequences for the film itself.

When I decided to become a movie actress, I had to leave the daily soap I was a part of. Although it was a difficult choice, I am incredibly proud of my bold move. Taking risks is an essential factor in the journey to success. At that time, the fundamentals of making it big in the movie business were unknown to me. Networking was a foreign concept to me, as I only had a small group of people with whom I enjoyed discussing movies and various aspects of life—my husband being at the top of that list. Despite being unable to attend social gatherings or parties for the past five or six years, my husband and I have made it a point to dedicate 20 or 30 minutes of our day to sit down and engage in heartfelt conversations about our feelings, emotions, past experiences, things that bother us, or how our day has been or will be. In one such conversation, I emphasized to him the importance of watching movies for an actor to prepare for a role and how crucial it is to establish connections within the industry to secure those roles in the first place. It's funny. Well, at least it was amusing when I first started, especially considering my extreme introversion. Throughout my school and college days, I preferred keeping to myself, possibly because I found that gossip irks me.

Before landing my first lead role in "Cyber Yugadol Nava Yuva Madhura Prema Kavyam," I had played several supporting roles. In one such movie, where I agreed to be a part of the film just because I badly needed money to pay our monthly debts, that role seemed decent enough. It was a screen-sharing experience with Mrs. Sudha Murthy and renowned actor Mr.Ananth Nag. I had to play an anchor's part in some school function scenes. Even though I have done lots of stage plays and television soaps, facing a camera for the film was different and new for me, too. With these veterans, I was a little nervous. I am an actor, and I demand a script beforehand. As actors, we should be familiar with our lines before facing the camera. For minor roles and low-budget movies, especially in those days, they don't care much except for the lead actors and well-known ones. *"Shwetha, please take your position on stage,"* said the director. *All veterans are busy getting all the attention; I was nobody that day.* *"Sir, can I get to see the script, please?"* I asked, *"Hey, haven't you given the script yet?"* the director shouted at the associate; he just nodded. *"Please take your lines. We have two minutes,"* said the director to me.

I saw the script, and it was an anchor's role; I had pages to memorize. It was an embarrassing day for me. I was a mess that whole day. And it shattered my confidence. I had left everything to do this? End of the day, when I happened to collect my remuneration of rupees two thousand five hundred, I wanted the land to be slit wide open, and I tried to drown deep down there.

However, many such incidents couldn't stop me from chasing my goals. I became stronger and stronger. I wasn't satisfied with those parts because I knew deep down that I was meant to be a lead actress. Unfortunately, due to my limited connections in the industry, I had to make do with whatever opportunities came my way. I longed to sing and dance on screen. That dream finally materialized in "AathmaSakshi," where I played a lead role with a negative shade. The entire team consisted of newcomers, and the experience was positive. The film was based on a short story, marking the first time I portrayed a lead character. I have heard countless motivational speakers discuss the importance of never giving up. Indeed, one must never surrender, especially when they are immensely passionate about something and have a dream to pursue. Perseverance is a virtue possessed by only a few, as the discouragement one faces can often feel insurmountable.

During those moments when nothing seems to work out and life appears dark and daunting, it's important to remember that night cannot persist forever. I recall those days—or years when my husband and I faced the worst circumstances. There were moments when I even contemplated ending my life due to the financial burdens we carried. I relied solely on my husband's income, and as he faced his challenges, we found ourselves drowning in debt. I didn't dare to confess this to my father, but fortunately, my mother came to my aid. She took me to my aunt and uncle, who helped us with our debt, which we later repaid. Offering assistance at the right time proved to be crucial. No matter what my situation was, I never compromised on my dreams. My husband, mother, and family were my pillars of strength. Even during the darkest times, expressing gratitude for what we have is essential.

Being thankful for the most minor things can propel us to the next level. The law of attraction truly worked for me during those days, as maintaining a positive attitude toward my dire circumstances opened doors to new opportunities. Trust me. I have witnessed and experienced it firsthand. As I began receiving offers for supporting roles in a few movies, I noticed that some individuals might mislead you for their benefit. They would approach you for what they claimed to be an essential role, only to reveal later that it was a supporting role. These experiences taught me to be more cautious and confident about my desires. Clarity of thought is essential.

During my struggle to enter films, I constantly approached many directors, filmmakers, producers, and a few from the film fraternity. Many of them requested an opportunity, and I faced nothing but straight rejection. Among all of these, the most terrifying was this process. I encountered a few of them, and they were always trying to mislead me forcibly. However, I was wise enough and strongly capable of understanding their intentions. I did not get carried away/fall into a trap, though. I was very sure about what I wanted, and it was crystal clear at the same time, and I was not desperate. I wonder how many innocents would fall into this trap and feel helpless.

Thus, my struggle during the initial days resembled a newborn's anxious crawl – I was trying to find people and resources I could hold on to as I wanted to stretch myself upwards and walk on my feet. What I cannot emphasize enough is that we assume our daughters won't have to be independent. We believe daughters can attempt to support their husband's preexisting resources and never be the breadwinner. However, the world is changing. Today, daughters have their own dreams, and we attempt to fulfill them by ourselves. I was lucky because the man of my life – my husband – was always by my side. There were hiccups, arguments, disagreements, and so much more along the way. Still, as long as there is dialogue, mutual respect, and unconditional love, these arguments become the pillars on which you build your life's foundation.

Telling my story in the form of this book has been an attempt to understand my decisions in life. The more I think about the past, the more I am confident that much of life has to do with accepting our shortcomings and pushing ourselves out of our comfort zone. Regardless, the fruits of my labor have been bittersweet, often sweet but sometimes sour. We walk through rain and shine to overcome these hindrances and cement our feet in our little corner of the world. I realized with time that both the Sun and the rain can become much more bearable with an umbrella. It is simple, but when it comes to acknowledging and overcoming our hurdles in life, we fail to seek help when we should. An umbrella can be our partner, family, and, most importantly, our financial and mental independence.

Please don't limit yourself; it is all in your mind! Be limitless.

7
STARDOM

Recently, I had the opportunity to serve as a jury member alongside esteemed filmmakers in a well-regarded newspaper's short film festival. I approached one of the filmmakers, expressing my interest in pursuing a career as a leading actress. Unfortunately, this particular filmmaker failed to see me as a "heroine" and instead offered me a minor supporting role that didn't align with my age at the time. Interestingly, this same individual was present as a fellow jury member. Out of the blue, he inquired whether I had altered my name or made any astrological adjustments to enhance my prospects in the industry. I couldn't help but laugh at his question, as I firmly disbelieve in such practices. I chose not to respond, dismissing the notion altogether.

There was a time when I approached an astrologer when nothing was working in my favor during my struggling days. My horoscope reader told me that entering the film industry would not be in my favor as it would not work in my case. Had I given up on that particular day, the book I am writing today would not have come to fruition. We hold the power to shape our destiny. Science, reason, logic, magic, and even calculations can all be advantageous, but only when we analyze and interpret them uniquely.

I acknowledge and embrace the idea that these tools can be effective for me, but only after I have thoroughly studied and applied them in a manner that suits my needs. It is uber important for us to be aware of our limitations, weaknesses, and strengths. I have realized that I am my greatest ally, and no one else understands the depth of my aspirations as I do. Only I possess the ability to strive towards my objectives and aspirations. When social media was still rising, platforms like Orkut and Facebook became popular networking sites, considered the "in thing" at the time. Although I wasn't particularly adept at social networking and preferred to limit my time in front of electronic devices, my husband created an account for me on these sites. Maintaining a social presence was essential as a public figure, whether through a dedicated team or personal effort if hiring professionals was not feasible.

I have realized how important it is to do what needs to be done rather than what you want to do. Adhering to the philosophy of prioritizing necessary tasks over personal desires, I ventured into social media. To my surprise, it proved beneficial. Despite already establishing myself in the industry through supporting roles in television dramas and films, my social media presence became an advantage. The director of the film 'Cyber Yugadol,' with whom I had previously worked on a TV soap, noticed my online presence and approached me for the heroine role. Here, I have to appreciate his broad-mindedness, as he didn't think twice before casting me in his movie as a lead, even though few others were skeptical as I was a married woman.

I was playing a college student's role. (and of course, it doesn't apply to male actors in this matter, is my point) so whether it is Mr. Simple Suni sir (SOLS film director) or Mr. Madhu Chandra (cyber yugadol film director), I got to be extremely thankful to a few of those who had considered me as a lead protagonist in their respective films even before I gave a massive blockbuster in the film industry. I have to appreciate their mindset.

While filming this (Cyber yugadol) movie, I recall an incident involving a female supporting character from the film crew who was intensely curious about my marital status. While my aunt accompanied me on set for a few days, this individual approached her, seeking information about my relationship status. Caught off guard and flustered, my aunt hastily responded that she was unaware of my marital status, although the answer seemed obvious.

Learning about this incident from my aunt at the end of the day ignited a fire within me. I took it upon myself to confront the inquisitive woman, determined to clarify her doubts. I also questioned whether she held the same level of curiosity regarding the male lead in the film. This experience left me wondering why women sometimes become their harshest critics and adversaries.

However, these trivial incidents did not deter me from pursuing my goals. I emerged triumphant by winning the prestigious Filmfare Award for Best Debutant for the same movie. I encountered the same lady at a mall shortly after the award announcement. Meeting her gaze, I proudly shared the news of my achievement. She offered a hesitant congratulations before swiftly moving on.

Upon reflection, I may now consider my response to be somewhat imprudent. Nevertheless, as a woman, it was crucial for me to remind others that attempting to undermine fellow women who strive to forge their paths is never acceptable. When one woman clears a path for herself, it undoubtedly paves the way for countless others.

I heard those words for the second time as I held the coveted Black Lady. The first time I won this prestigious award was for my role in the 2014 film "Fair and Lovely," where I portrayed the character of a sex worker. Overwhelmed by the exhilaration of this victory, I glanced across the stage. I realized that many people in the audience had endured countless hardships to establish their names and get an invitation to this esteemed award show. I, too, was no exception to the agony of striving as an outsider to make my mark in the film industry.

However, another challenge weighed heavily on my mind – I was a married woman. A married woman entering the film industry as a leading protagonist was deemed unthinkable and absurd, especially in commercial films. Being recognized as a heroine in such movies was an accomplishment, and I take great pride in achieving it!

Watching films like Mr. Satyajit Ray's, Mr. Mrinal Sen's, and Mr. Puttanna Kanagal's "Gejje Pooje" (and other intellectual movies) profoundly impacted me. They ignited my curiosity about the stories women had to share. I delved into more movies, such as "Sophie's Choice," "Umrao Jaan," "Out of Africa," and "Frida." Although I enjoyed these films immensely, their narratives haunted me. Movies with thought-provoking concepts, those that questioned the realities of the world, and ones that truly showcased the essence of art fascinated me. Even after all these years in the industry, I continue to derive immense pleasure from watching women-oriented movies, regardless of the language. However, my cinematic preferences were not confined to a single genre.

I couldn't pinpoint a specific movie genre that captivated me entirely. Unfortunately, the industry had a problem with this as well. They preferred categorizing individuals, forcing them to choose between being fans of commercial or art films. There was no room for an in-between, and deviating from these predefined labels often resulted in rejection.

As a newcomer to the industry, this notion was incredibly frustrating. It forced me to choose between my diverse interests and demanded that I restrict myself to a single genre. The worst part was that these industry hotshots would dismiss you if you didn't conform to the labels they imposed or if you didn't fit their preconceived notions.

We must know that society is filled with people ready to offer harmful and unnecessary advice to divert us from our goals. I vividly remember a respected person in the industry advising me to stop having opinions about films and to abandon my habit of jotting down and reviewing movies.

Unfortunately, I succumbed to their suggestion and stopped taking notes. However, continuing this practice would have greatly benefited me when researching for future roles. It's time for me to rekindle this habit, considering how times have changed and how the industry has evolved with respect to transparency with the advent of social media.

Numerous talented young girls are eagerly waiting for an opportunity to enter this industry. Talent alone is just a tiny part of what it takes to succeed. Building connections and knowing the right people to help bring your dreams to fruition is equally crucial. In the early days of my film career as a lead, I had the opportunity to shoot abroad for the first time. We traveled to Bali, Indonesia, and although the experience was beautiful, I also felt a sense of fatigue and sadness. Shooting for 16 to 17 hours a day took its toll, and it saddened me. I realized that it didn't seem the way it looked when we used to read about other big-budget film teams enjoying foreign locations while shooting.

As it was a song shoot and I had some costume changes and other basic help, I requested one lady to accompany me. Still, the budget was tight, and I had to request my costume designer, who happened to be a female, to hop in instead of a makeup artist. I could manage (well, in this matter, I had zero experience). The first time our team was traveling internationally, a couple of guys were eagerly waiting to have a drink (as they serve wine/hot drinks in the flight). They were super excited, and as soon as the flight took off, they started drinking alcohol. Our bad, they just puked the whole way till landing. It was hilarious, and obviously, they didn't dare try it while returning to India. Let me share my experience as I risked by taking a designer instead of a makeup artist as we couldn't accommodate one more person; I looked yellow the whole song ...hahaha ... I didn't know much about makeup back then, and I messed up. But, anyway ... all I got to understand is these are the basic amenities and facilities a female artist demands; where is a caravan/vanity van? Female assistants like me, many women face this, and I have had bad experiences even with a female director in this matter, to be frank enough. It is sad that even today, we hear that these needs are considered a demand, and they consider this a burden, which has to be a significant shift in this way of thinking. Let's try to take a more professional approach to this.

Nonetheless, I felt like I was inching closer and closer to my dream. The experience of shooting a song in a foreign country was simply extraordinary.

Honestly, I agreed to be a part of "Simple Agi Ondh Love Story" without fully understanding the movie's theme. I signed on with hesitation because I didn't grasp the story, but I was offered a lead role, and the team seemed decent to work with. One of the main reasons was the monetary benefits involved. I never stopped hustling and continuously forged my path. Despite facing rejection and lacking connections in the industry, I remained determined. In the beginning, I reached out to the people I knew and managed to gather information about a few filmmakers. I would wait for hours outside their offices just for a minute of their time, attempting to convince them to cast me.

I remember one incident with another filmmaker who questioned my persona and claimed I lacked the aura and charisma to be a leading lady in a movie. However, when the "Simple Agi Ondh Love Story" trailer was released, it unexpectedly went viral. Back then, social media wasn't as prominent in our daily lives. Overnight, my Facebook followers skyrocketed from 5,000 to

80,000. It was a phenomenal and unexpected turn of events, especially for someone like me, whose worth had been doubted. I wasn't allowed to showcase my talent, and rejection was already predetermined due to being an outsider.

There is one more exciting incident from my struggling days. I went to meet a highly influential film director. After several hours, I was finally allowed to talk to him. However, before I could make my case, he questioned, "Why do you want to be an actor? Why not be a director, a scriptwriter, or a technician?" I was speechless, unable to provide a proper response. I got up and left the building without expressing myself adequately. Countless questions raced through my mind, and I felt deeply offended. This director not only rejected me but also suggested that I should consider an alternative career path. It felt like he was asking me to give up on my dreams. This rejection affected me greatly, pushing me into grief and constant darkness.

Now, I understand that success takes time, and one must work hard while focusing solely on the efforts required in the present. The outcome is part of the future, beyond our control, but we should always feel like we can give our best and put forth our utmost efforts. The feeling of defeat may be stronger than the sense of accomplishment, but knowing that we gave our all to the challenge brings much-needed satisfaction. I often find myself revisiting "Simple Agi Ondh Love Story," not only because it was my first major blockbuster or because of its box office success but primarily because of the experience it provided. Everyone gave their best on that set, and a group of newcomers came together to make the film happen. The passion displayed on that set was indescribable because each person was striving to achieve their dreams. We celebrated the film's 100-day run, and it wasn't just us shedding tears of joy; I even witnessed a theater owner shedding tears because his theater was packed with audiences. "Simple Agi Ondh Love Story" made me a star, with fans waiting outside my house in crowds to meet me. It was like a dream for which I am immensely grateful.

I find myself contemplating what the people in the industry think of me now, especially those who rejected me or offered me compromises that would guarantee me a role. This fear led me to bring my husband to these meetings, although his presence by my side didn't yield any offers in the movie business. One day after SOLS' success, I and the film team were sitting in this very famous outdoor café in Bangalore, giving an interview to a newspaper. A journalist from a leading newspaper, Times of India, was sitting in front of me. Very casually, she asked in between the interviews: "So Shwetha, can you share what the characteristics you would look for in a man of your dreams ?" Suddenly, the whole atmosphere turned to silence, as our team was aware that I was married, and this was a new concept for the journalist. She didn't even expect that I could be married, as no new heroine in the history of Indian cinema was married before entering the industry. So, it is not her fault.

Somehow, I felt awkward confronting this question. I became silent, and in this instance, I couldn't respond. The entire cafe where the interview took place fell into complete silence. Even my film team was still determining if it was their place to answer this question, so they remained quiet. Everyone was taken aback, and my facial expression changed as the conversation around us stopped. Concerned, the journalist asked if I was okay. And I reassured them that everything was fine but disclosed that I was married and my husband was indeed my dream man. Subsequently, the journalist, being kind enough, chose not to pursue that line of questioning further. However, at that moment, I felt I had committed a crime simply by getting married. Why was it so difficult for them? And why did it trouble me as well? These questions haunted me and filled me with apprehension about the future ahead. This was a decade ago; now, we are happy that society welcomes such a broad-minded mindset. Even though this is high time, we completely accept it.

Having said this, I would like to add here that in life, to bring the change in the mindset takes time, and if you are on the other side of the journey, definitely try and enjoy the trip no matter how hard it looks, rather than worrying about reaching the destination. It helps.

8
CHANGING DIAPERS

Even after giving a blockbuster movie like "Simple Aag Ondhu Love Story," the fact is that I did not get many offers since all the attention was on marital status. Whatever I got, I chose a couple of women-oriented subjects. Luckily, both films did well at the box office, and my role was critically acclaimed for my acting skills. Even though my career graph was at its peak, my biological clock was ticking as a woman, and I had to take time for my obligations.

I decided not to take up any more projects and take my personal life more seriously – it was still a perplexing time for me. I faced a lot of pressure after the success of my last film before the sabbatical; I was going through a difficult phase because of the heavy publicity expectations. Meanwhile, my relatives and friends were expanding their families and started pointing fingers at me. Society works on the principles of envy and fulfillment – it was difficult to know if I envied their successful family lives or if they envied my successful career. Regardless, I walked on and continued my journey – one where I was determined to find a delicate balance between my job and my family. Every step of the way, I realized that this was easier said than done. Such a delicate balance requires sacrifice and communication – it seeks the effort and compromise of both partners. Thankfully, despite the harshness of the circumstances we were in – I was happy to learn I was pregnant.

I was ready to accept this new addition to my life with full fervor and love. I remember when my husband and I decided to extend the family, it was not easy for the first couple of months, as I started getting lots of free advice, complaints, comments, suggestions, and whatnot from a very close circle too, and that time I was even promoting one of my movies, where there was this mouth to mouth spread of a word about my conceiving news. It was a disaster, as I could hear a lot of rumors too!! It was hard. Every woman trying to conceive will understand the state of my mind then. One day, I decided that no matter what happened, I would face society boldly and happily. It is my body and my life, after all. We wanted to conceive naturally; if it didn't happen, we were ready to leave the wish to become parents and move on with our lives. But, one fine morning, when I took a pregnancy test, it showed positive. We cross-checked with the gynecologist, and the news was confirmed. We all were happy at our home.

The first few months of my pregnancy were filled with nausea and physical discomfort. Moreover, I was still receiving invites to attend events as a chief guest. I had decided not to reveal the pregnancy news so soon. I was receiving offers to inaugurate award shows, and I also received a proposal for a film. I had to reject the movie without a reasonable explanation because we had decided to wait before revealing the news to the world. The director was initially upset, but when the news was confirmed about my pregnancy, it was clear why I chose to reject the film. Despite the joy this pregnancy brought me, I also witnessed difficulties dealing with this life-changing experience as a part of the film industry. It is difficult for women in the industry to experience this.

I was giving an interview for a news channel, as it was something new for the news channels to record a program with a pregnant heroine; back then, it was taboo to be in the limelight of your pregnancy.

Interviewer: "Ma'am, do you want a boy child or a girl child?". "Oh!! Just a healthy baby and I'll be happier if it is a girl, to be honest." I said: But I wouldn't say I liked the question, though, and I was trying to be kind, so I didn't reach much to this one, but the next one.... Interviewer: "Ma'am, would you like to continue with the acting profession after giving birth?"

"I might take some time to heal physically, but why would I quit acting? That, too, after all these struggles to be where I am today? And I wonder why actresses have to tackle such questions. Why don't we ask an actor the same if he is about to become a father? Except for the duration of physical healing for actresses, parenting is something that plays an equal part for both parents. And it applies to actors who are fathers as well?"

I said, but I knew that I'd be edited for my safety only, as Kannada media have always helped us not to ruin our image amongst our audience. They knew these statements would be a little hard for the mass audience to digest. Maybe we need more such collective mindsets to bring about some changes in the mass audience.

Ours is public life, and all our decisions are judged – no matter how much we try to be "correct." Moreover, we cannot escape this scrutiny – this is part and parcel of the profession we chose to be. Slowly, with time, the joy of becoming a mother overtook all my thoughts and fears. I no longer cared for the world – I could switch off from the outer world to rejuvenate and recharge. This is an important exercise that all human beings must indulge in. During such a rigorous and challenging time – the experience of a public pregnancy – this switch that helped me shut out the world was the best thing I could have wanted. Indeed, in this world of an overabundance of information and opinion, we must find ways to sit with ourselves, our loved ones, and our families and be – without the pressure of our job or future.

Somehow, I had always wished to travel abroad when I got pregnant and wanted the international fight boarding experience, as we had heard so many special incidences regarding special treatment with all the special facilities provided for pregnant women in fights during international travels. I used to visualize it innocently and wholeheartedly. There were no reasons, no such opportunities, and no financial independence where I could have afforded it. But I didn't stop dreaming as it didn't cost a cent for me, and my mind used to be in a happy mode in my imaginary world.

This was not new for me; I have been a dreamer since childhood; who knows, that is helping me keep my aura aligned to attract what I want!

Suddenly, one evening, my husband returned from the office and told me I had received an email from Qatar Kannada Sangha; they wanted to invite me to Qatar to felicitate me for my achievements. I couldn't believe this news. I was in my second trimester, so I got permission from my gynecologist to fly abroad. Just then, my nausea was down, and then my dream experience was incredible. This incident is extraordinary because it helps me believe in miracles even now when I sometimes feel things are not going well. Being an artist, through art, we wanted to showcase our joy and love of becoming a mother to the world. So, we decided to paint my baby bump. This was a very new cultural shock to our audience, and I was the first heroine from the Kannada film industry to try it. Did anyone mock me? Probably, but I'm a woman, and motherhood is a unique gift bestowed upon me; why should I be shy about it? Having a womb is a blessing; nourishing a life inside it is a feeling so mesmerizing.

My husband and I wanted to welcome our little one creatively, so we took the plunge; however, my choices somehow provoked unwanted attention. I was criticized not only by the male audience but also by my female followers on social media. After I recognized their limited span of thought, we didn't give much attention to the negative comments. But I remember getting personal messages from a lot of supporters, too. One of them was a doctor who shared my name as well. She mentioned that she was inspired by my post about belly painting. She decided to immortalize her bump with art just like I did. Suddenly, I could feel my messenger having a positive vibe. After spending so many years in this industry, I know now what irks people the most. Revolution. It is more painful to the prick if a woman instigates the revolution. My motto as an individual is to make a change as an artist. Moreover, as a mother, being loud and clear about my beliefs and values is vital. I want my child to be proud of my actions and glad to be part of my life.

Motherhood and its connotations have significantly impacted me across various stages of my life. Whether it be in dealing with my mother's ideas of motherhood as a child or the question of my abilities as a mother – it is a phenomenon none of us can avoid. Becoming a mother was a decision controlled by various factors – my relationship with my partner, my career, my upbringing, and societal expectations – everything had a massive role in my experience. Of course, despite the pious idea of motherhood, I encountered a fair share of unbelievable behavior toward me after my pregnancy. I am reminded of encounters with a famous actor and his reaction to my pregnancy. After having my child, during my maternity break, I was hounded by television offers. People ask me why I have not considered working for soaps, television series, and reality shows.

Furthermore, they are concerned about whether I am rejecting these offers or not getting any deals in the first place. People believe our career decisions are based solely on money and fame. People around me are curious about me not obtaining lucrative deals or not networking enough with the right people. I am torn between these questions because it has always been about personal preferences. The world of television has built me; hence, it will always have unconditional love and respect in my heart. However, my passion for movies has built its course over time., I prefer to work in the cinema; I have yet to take up offers from television. After my daughter was born, I had to take a break to rest and recuperate. My relaxation is a personal choice that I am exercising for my well-being. However, artists enjoy being in front of the camera.

Regardless of where and how we started in life, all artists desire to experience the world of a "protagonist" – a main character for whom the story is designed. I learned early on that I wanted to become a protagonist of my life and work; hence, I decided not to compromise my choices and aspire for what is best for me. Moreover, all this chatter about whether or not I should work for television today reminds me of when I first started working. I never had to face the brunt of such questions because television was the most essential form of media when I started. Television arrived in India in the 80s and slowly developed its presence in the news and entertainment world. There were channels dedicated to community health, the responsibilities of citizens, traffic and road safety, and entertainment. After a rough start, the television world expanded immensely over the decades, bringing new avenues for artists like me. Prasar Bharti expanded and brought in Doordarshan and All India Radio, creating a new platform for family entertainment in India. Today, millions of Indians own and consume television content day and night. Furthermore, the internet works as a vast archive of old television content, ensuring the content has a life beyond the expiration date. These statistics and advancements remind me of the scale at which actors perform – our audiences are ever-increasing and consuming content at high rates at any given time. Over the years, I have embraced the pressure and responsibility of performing for our audiences. It is an honor to join television's journey in this country. Growing up with trauma is difficult; only we can help ourselves and heal it. I found a way to deal with my trauma – I found it in my family and my career.

Today, I acknowledge the burden of the past but also celebrate the joys of the past. Through a delicate balance of acceptance and evolution, I can move forward and challenge myself as a woman. No matter how hard your journey seems or how evil people are, it would help if you channel your sadness into your strength. You must mold your fears and anxieties into something that is strengthening – something that can help you move on. Learning lessons and being vigilant about things that can pull you down is essential. Motherhood is a natural part of our lives – it is our choice.

It is the responsibility of the film industry to take cognizance of the experiences of to-be and new mothers. I had decided very early on not to compromise on my ideals and principles simply because I took a two-year break because of my pregnancy. I would never give up on my dreams only because I took maternity leave. Unfortunately, it is rare to see women play the role of protagonists after becoming mothers in the Film Industry. There are only so many actresses who would have done it. I wish to be an actor who plays diverse roles and raises the bar for women wanting to act after expanding their families – I want to raise the bar. I want more women to come after me and achieve more than me – despite the obstacles they have faced in their personal lives. An artist should not be judged for anything other than her craft.

She should be respected if she is an artist and good for the part. I am grateful for the change in my attitude that has allowed me to embrace this vision. I am also thankful that society is changing for the better – in resonance with my life choices. I have been able to work in three films after my pregnancy – essaying the role of a protagonist. What's more, I also have two more projects in the making! All after my baby was born, who is now five years old and an unshakeable part of my life. I have covered for the five years I did not work for within my first year after my pregnancy! Earlier, I would do one project every year. This journey has been the biggest motivation in my life – it has taught me the importance of staying strong and moving ahead no matter the circumstance. I was sure I wanted to be a lead actor in the films.

I come from a family where my mother was denied work because she would wear sleeveless blouses to work! Overcoming these biases within my family and myself was the real task – augmented with the help of a magical switch that enabled me to shut out the world's noise and concentrate on the people who matter to me. I have learned with time that we need to get something right the first time. As much as we want to test the limits of our abilities and aspire to excel as quickly as possible – good things take time. It took me several years of undoing, relearning, and rebirthing to arrive at a point where my life is comfortable. I learned that a seeker's fundamental quality is to be willing to explore and experience life in all its colors. All you have to do is be courageous and face off your fears!

9
IF I WERE A BOY

On the film sets, we were shooting for a song sequence, and the choreographer, with his female dance assistant, showed us the steps, where the hero had to give a peck on my cheeks. Somehow, the actor was reluctant, and he asked me in private with a very hesitating tone,

"Shwetha, madam, will your husband not mind if we do this sequence?" As soon as I heard this, I burst out of laughter. Then I asked him, *"Sir, won't your wife feel bad about this?!"*

He took it lightly, and we continued the shooting. This might sound funny, but trust me. I have often been asked about this topic. Especially after having my baby, I encounter questions like, will I continue doing romantic movies? Will I have to be more choosey in selecting my character? Will I be able to do intimate scenes? Why don't they ask the same of a man? I tend to picture myself as a boy in every situation in life. How would the situation be for the same?

I have so many incidents to share in this particular chapter; in every such situation, if I see myself as a man and want to imagine the same situation, I am sure the reaction or reply would be different/the opposite. Once, I called a well-known director who is our good friend, and I even worked with him to invite him to my film's special screening. I was in the movie as the lead protagonist. He politely rejected my invitation and said to my face that he couldn't come as the director or the producers should invite him to the show.

I was left wondering, 'If I were a man/hero,' he definitely wouldn't have said that to me. Why is the mindset so? Feminism, to me, is the advocacy of women's rights and opportunities based on equality for all genders. It is about respecting all women's experiences, identities, knowledge, and struggles – and striving to empower all women so they can realize their full rights. Feminism is about choice. Patriarchy means "rule of the father" in ancient Greek. It is a social structure in which men have more power and privilege than women in all aspects of society.

I have been asked about feminism – whether I am a feminist or not. I sound like a feminist, and people generally take my opinions seriously. I am getting stronger and stronger as a human in knowing my rights. Feminism is a vast topic – and we can never limit this conversation to a few aspects. I am concerned about how feminism has shaped my life. I wish to understand the chaos of my life from the prism of feminism. I seek fundamental rights for myself in the film industry.

Slow and steady wins the race – is what they say. After spending some time in the industry, I was slowly making my path. After years of waiting and working, a film of mine worked very well at the box office. It was what would be called a "success" in every sense. The people loved it; it did well at the box office, and the audience appreciated my role. However, after this enormous success, I started getting recognized and began another tough life ordeal. I was exposed to the harsh realities of the world, to this unfair life. I had no choice but to accept the bitter truth of society. All the cruel biases a woman faces in every step of her life were amplified now that I was famous. It was a chaotic time in my life. Still, with the help of my spirituality and dedication to myself, I began my journey to overcome it. I was on the path toward finding my authentic self.

It was empowering and inspirational, and there was something energetically palpable about this journey. It catapulted a shift in me, in my thinking. It helped me in disrupting the old and stagnant patterns of my life. Self-growth is the most essential part of anyone's journey. We should work on our purpose and try to break free from all the false notions we built for ourselves under the world's influence. We must identify the illusions and hold on to the reality of our lives, embrace it, and let it heal us. During tough times, these moments you spend caring for yourself help you overcome stress and anxiety. I am reminded of one such turbulent time after the success of my film. I was watching this show where one of my previous co-actors was interviewed. I watched the interview for a long time after it aired. They were asking him silly, light-hearted questions. During the interview, they told him the names of fruits and vegetables as a funny game. They asked him which actors he was reminded of after hearing their names. Which actor comes to mind when thinking of a "potato?" My co-actor took my name when he was asked that. The interviewer asked him why he thought of Potato and Shwetha Srivatsav together. The actor confessed that he thought of me because I was pregnant and resembled a potato. Listening to this answer, an apparent incident of body shaming of a pregnant woman, was a very disheartening experience.

Society idolizes this actor and considers him the next big star of the Kannada film industry. I felt pathetic after listening to this conversation and very under-confident. Returning to the film industry after my pregnancy was a very daunting experience. In such seemingly minuscule ways, the world reminded me that I was a woman, a married woman, and now a mother – trying to make her journey in a world of cinema dominated by men and their camaraderie.

Furthermore, after the success of my films, very few team members would congratulate me, the heroine of these films. I recall an instance when a movie I was a huge part of became successful.

Every person from the film industry called and congratulated the director and the ship's captain, as they should, no doubt about it. The hero of the film was celebrated as well. They took the technicians' names, but very few people congratulated me on my participation in the movie. I was on screen as much as the male actor, but my participation was neglected in comparison. Why? It is not about me, Shwetha Srivatsav – it is about the neglect and lack of acknowledgment of women in cinema. The movie was promoted for a long time, but after a point, the hero stopped touring with me. They take the heroine of a film for granted. They felt the response I was getting from the audience was huge – they could tell that my engagement played a huge role in the film's success. However, the attitude of the creators was that I should be grateful for the opportunity.

The hero is never told such things; his participation is celebrated and heralded as the most significant contribution to the film. This discrimination is rampant in contemporary times as well. For most movies, the contribution of women is the same. Heroines are expected to make physical compromises for all their roles – big female stars worldwide have spoken about this. Meryl Streep, Salma Hayek, Emma Thomson, Smitha Patil, Shabana Azmi, and many more such strong female voices have spoken up about the lack of respect for women contributors in cinema. To this day, I am puzzled by such incidents; how am I, as an actor, supposed to react to them? It is difficult to speak up for yourself when so much is at stake – the success of your films and the kind of roles you get in the future depend on how you are portrayed in public.

After I gained success, I realized that the nature of the audience's reaction is very different for men and women. I can't say if it is good or bad because I am reminded that these differences are "human nature." However, it does not change the fact that I feel uncomfortable with how I am perceived. Men in the industry have a "boys' club," where they are very comfortable with each other and stand up for each other. On the other hand, I am a woman and a married woman at that. I was declared "old enough" to play a heroine's role in a movie, kept in isolation. In regional language cinema, there is an immense disparity between men and women in the industry. I have been active in the industry for over 15 years and feel horrified by the disparity.

Furthermore, when I met men in the film industry – my encounter with the real world – I understood the privilege of being raised by my parents. Their upbringing made sure I could never think too little of anyone – respect was a fundamental value to live with. However, several men in the industry fail to understand that their behavior toward women can be distasteful and oppressive. Disrespectful behavior is normalized in the form of jokes that belittle women. Our needs and requirements are perceived as "differences" – labeled as obstacles to "creative freedom." My marriage and motherhood were perceived as obstacles – this was not the same for many men in the industry. These experiences propelled me to write this book.

There is this unsubstantiated theory that feminism falls into three categories for men – men who are proud feminists and seek equal opportunities for women in the workplace, decision-making, domestic labor, and raising children. The second category of men who do not have a strong inclination either way – the social position of their partner informs their opinions. If the partner asserts their rights, he accepts; if she does not, he does not try to change them. The third category of men tends to uphold patriarchy; they believe we need patriarchy to maintain the world order. Such men actively encourage discrimination and are agitated when anyone challenges their views.

I think such a categorization is very apt – I have encountered such men, and my experiences have been shaped by how they wish to exercise their right to accept or reject my rights. Hence, despite men's many good intentions, the world can be problematic for women because we never know what qualifies as good for them. A man would believe he is good, and his actions are good despite the category he belongs to – he could be a good feminist man, he could be an excellent complacent man who would never disturb the ways of a woman's life, or he could be a "good" patriarchal man who is convinced that his way of life is the only way to be, for everyone's peace.

Moreover, there are many ignorant women in the world, too. When bound to a household or specific gender-based roles – we often fail to experience the world in its multiplicity. I was expected to be a mother, and I only became a mother after having my child. Had I not challenged myself after experiencing the bliss of motherhood, the world would have accepted my decision and not questioned the parameters stopping me from leaving that comfort zone. As a mother, I was the apple of everyone's eye – a young woman who brought so much happiness into the lives of so many people. However, my happiness can have multiple sources and multiple outlets as well. I am very perturbed by the question of feminism – I enjoy watching films and consuming media about women's empowerment. They seem to stir the dialogues in my head – questions I ask myself about the status of women worldwide and the entertainment industry. Women are always expected to succumb to certain practices, fight for their rights, accept failure, and grapple with that unfortunate realization.

When I look around, these differences boggle my mind, and even the changes that have occurred over the decades are unsatisfactory. Moreover, I wonder why this is trickier in the entertainment industry. I firmly believe that unity among women and mutual support are crucial. Suppose we desire more movies with women in leading roles. In that case, we need women to actively attend theaters and support films that tell stories by and for women. The impetus for such projects must come from women themselves.

Unfortunately, this is often not the case. Furthermore, based on common consensus, men would be more interested in watching stories centered around women than men. However, there needs to be more male viewership for such content. This paradox arises because societal conditioning and inherent biases have led men and some women to overlook or be less entertained by stories about women. This phenomenon is particularly pronounced in the world of film. This ongoing debate about equality for women has consistently hindered conversations surrounding female athletes, actors, and other public figures who are questioned about their ability to attract audiences and generate revenue at the same level as their male counterparts.

Women must assert their presence as audience members and within the production realm to bring about a meaningful shift. Women must make their voices heard loudly and clearly to challenge the existing norms and biases. American writer, actor, and activist Jen Richards said, 'I rarely meet men in real life as extraordinary as the ones in films, and rarely see women in films as extraordinary as the ones I know in real life.' In this industry, women need to support and uplift one another. By actively engaging with and promoting media representing our lives and experiences, we can strive for a more inclusive and equitable entertainment industry. This collective effort will require overcoming societal conditioning and biases shaping our preferences. Ultimately, working together can create a future where women's stories are given the attention, appreciation, and financial support they deserve.

For such a shift to occur, women must make their presence felt loud and clear in the audience and the production room! In addition, when it comes to marriages, women are given the liberty to choose what they wish to do. However, earlier, let's say even fifteen years ago – such liberty was a privilege. As soon as I finished college, I was pressured to settle down. The meaning of "settle" had various connotations. Thankfully, for my family, this meant the possibility of marriage and the need to find a suitable career for myself. Of course, joining the film industry was a big no for a young woman. On the professional end, men and women are expected to overcome their shortcomings and climb the ladder of their choices as soon as possible.

In the hustle and bustle of achieving our dreams – marriage can be a significant drawback for women. Men are supposed to be responsible for being the bread-winning members of the family. However, they do not face the brunt of marriage and its responsibilities as much as women do. After their marriage, it is difficult for women to do something they like and enjoy. Even in the world of filmmaking, the kind of subjects we choose to work with are predominately male-dominated. We do not come across stories centered around women or their experiences. The huge hits, the commercially well-received films, are all about men, especially in the Kannada film industry (the statistics would be slightly different, but the same is true for Indian films and world films in general). The film industry is an influential medium – it has a significant impact on the lives of people.

It is about society and the people in power in the film industry. It is not just about me or the few talented actresses across the industry – the commercial industry has a different approach toward men and women.

The posters consist of men looking larger than life, holding a cigarette. These images make men appear to be significantly more important than women in this world. Such codes translate into the power dynamics we see in our households. Men eat the food that is cooked for them and leave, whereas women are supposed to clean up the mess and make sure everything in the house is in accordance with the men. Hence, men continue to live a life full of self-centered impulses. In contrast, women are constantly put down, unable to live with their heads held high. Such a difference in their ways of life is seen across so many families in the form of traditions and habits.

For the longest time, I was in despair because I could not gauge why I could not climb the ladder of success despite my efforts. I questioned my acting abilities, but it was not the case because my performances were appreciated. Accepting the length and breadth of discrimination worldwide took me a while. I got movie offers, but all the roles seemed similar; I realized I was typecasted. More than twenty to thirty film offers were for the same kind of character – identical to the ones I had portrayed and received a lot of accolades for. The dialogues and script were so ironically similar for all offers that I felt caged in my success. I did not want to do the same role for the rest of my career. I was typecasted for a "bold" role, and the audience appreciated my dialogue. Still, they were pretty different from the kind of dialogues other women get in the cinema. I am so thankful to the film's director and the film's team for giving me the opportunity to essay a bold and entertaining character. However, despite how much I enjoyed the role, I did not want to do the same role over and over again.

I continued to get roles that revolved around bold dialogues; many of these characters were sex workers. I was happy to essay the character. However, I just realized why all the roles I was offered were similar. My well-wishers told me this was the case because such roles were difficult to perform, and I could pull it off. It was a compliment to me that I was offered such a role. However, I was apprehensive about the crew and how they would treat the character in the film. I did not want to be a tokenistic presence in the movie; I wanted a vital and powerful role. An actor's character must be respected, no matter how big or small the role is. I gave up and took up one such role; it had been long since my last successful film. I wanted to make the most of the tide of success I was afloat on so that my work could survive the test of time. Because I put in the effort and showed my mettle, I stayed in the competition and succeeded. The role I accepted was perfect; it was treated very well. It did reasonably well at the box office. However, the audience had a lot more expectations of me. It was very difficult to process the production and aftermath of the film. The film was a psychological thriller with a love story –

I did not receive any roles for softer characters. Creators of more significant films like romantic comedies said they did not want good actors. Instead, they wanted conventional-looking and glamorous actors. Despite putting myself out there, I continued to ask myself why I did not get big roles in big movies. I realized this was because men drove most films, and those roles centered around them. Lead protagonists always want to project themselves as superior. If women contributors ask for their rights, the creators consider it a threat and suppress dissent. The only way out was to create a platform and sell my brand. It is a tough pill to swallow, but at the end of the day, we, as actors, have to nurture our talent and our brand. It is important to keep market expectations, competition, audience reactions, film criticism, and career goals in mind. In the middle of this chaos, there were also a few silver linings.

I recall receiving a unique opportunity to perform at a prominent film award show. I was young and new to the industry and missed the opportunity. I failed in my attempt to use this opportunity to climb the ladder. Like a ladder, this opportunity was right before me, but I did not know what to do with it. Was I supposed to climb it? How was I supposed to climb it if I had never seen it before? Would someone help me? My ignorance and questions paralyzed me, and I did not mint the opportunity for what it was worth in my career. I cannot blame others, but in hindsight, I did not know enough to forge my path. I feel despair when I recall such missed opportunities from my life and career. However, in this journey with myself, I have understood we can never blame the world for not serving us. No matter what the world does, how it treats you, no matter what your gender is, whether you are married or young or old – one must know that all these issues can be overcome. We can all create wonders for ourselves.

My journey reminds me that all obstacles can be overcome, and we can all carve our corners in the world. I have realized that I feel pathetic when I blame others for any disturbance. The blame is followed by helplessness, which is not a pleasant feeling at all. People might be terrible; they might create obstacles in my journey, but I do not want to complain about the same. There is good and evil in the world; it is up to us to decide what to focus on and where we want to spend our energy. Every time I see myself walk into a spiral of worry, I tell myself – stop waiting for others to make you feel loved, unique, and wanted. It would be best if you took charge of it alone. You have done it before, and you can do it again.

Unlike in other industries and careers, an actor must always balance social norms, the professional front, and personal lives. An actor must always show confidence because any sign of vulnerability can make you an outsider, something every actor fights hard not to be. Yet, an actor is blessed with the admiration they crave, the respect that any other professional receives. When I decided to join the film industry, everyone I shared this thought with looked confused. Some even took it up a notch and expressed their disgust. I was very perplexed as to why there is this negative perception of the industry, especially about the women in the industry, whereas men are glorified. Someone reading this might think I am being too sensitive and reading into the situation or complaining when I should be more thankful. I am grateful for everything I have been blessed with. I will keep working towards fulfilling people's expectations, but something stops me. It's a single question: why is being an artist looked down upon?

I would not like to associate myself with any of the '-isms' because I don't know what it is, but from what I can understand is that these '-isms' cannot be defined and described because there is no concrete meaning. My ideas of equality might not relate to someone else's, which is fine. Hence, I will not say I fit into one box. Yet, I understand the need for equality and for me to raise my voice and talk about gendered inequality. Indeed, some actors are not treated well. Being a part of this industry is looked down upon, but being a female is further frowned upon. We are often treated as trophies in the industry, people who have no other purpose but to be a thing, an object that is perfect in every possible way and fulfills people's fantasies. It was tough making a name for myself, even more so because I was married. Every producer who rejected me stated their ridiculous reasons, and some even tried to comfort me, giving me false hopes. Yet, my soul was being bogged down and crushed every day because this was what I wanted to be and pursue. I love my husband and am thankful for our marriage, yet it was a problem if I wanted to become an actor. Why can I not be married and pursue a career simultaneously? Men do it all the time. So, why can a woman not do the same?

Gender discrimination or gender bias is prevalent in the film industry as much as in any other industry. Most female actors will argue and say that it exists in greater detail. The men are worshiped and have dedicated fan bases that will do or die for them. Still, a female actor is a thing of desire and often objectified. We are always expected to be well-dressed and look perfect regardless of the weather or our mental health situation.

We have to be dolled up. Female actors are also not encouraged to have opinions about their roles, the characters they play, the costumes they are supposed to wear, and certainly not about the plot and story. Female actors are supposed to be models of what patriarchy imagines an ideal woman to be like. A female actor has to go through a lot, both mentally and physically, since everyone has a set standard of beauty. However unrealistic it may be, everyone wants to be close enough to achieve it.

I have seen that in events where male actors are called along with female actors, the male actors are constantly called upon first. Why? Irrespective of their success and time in the industry, they are called upon first. The mic is always given to them first, and the female artists are ignored. This is mainly because the men in our film industry are given more importance.

Very early in my career, I overlooked this discrimination. I thought this was the case for everyone, irrespective of gender. But as soon as I enjoyed fame after 'Simple Agi Ondh Love Story,' I realized the difference. I was invited to several promotions and events upon releasing my major hit film. Being a rookie in the industry, I was thrilled to attend these events, but my happiness would not last long. In one such event, the male actor accompanying me spoke about essential issues in the industry.

I am grateful to him for also appreciating my work. Yet, the organizers never passed the mic to me. Even after the senior actors were done speaking, after everyone was done speaking, I was never given a chance to hold the microphone, let alone say something to the people. Even though this act of bias was a long time ago and is arguably a minimal issue compared to many other problems, it still matters. It mattered to that newcomer who had been rejected quite a few times for ridiculous reasons, humiliated by various folks, and whose integrity had been questioned several times.

The social unevenness among men and women in the industry must be solved. A discussion of the needs of a woman should be put forth. Incidents like this remind me that I should not be a part of creating this bias; that is the least I can do on my part. People who instigate such behavior and prejudice are ignorant. I want to disassociate and condemn this behavior as a woman, especially in this industry. I will try my hardest not to be like that.

In every stage of my life from childhood until today, I often question myself – "What if I were a boy?" and every time, I know for sure the situation and attention would have been much better and much more deserving than what I have received as a girl.

Someone else is coming to tell you what to do. How to do it. All you've got, are you? You must be the one to take that step. Take actions. Be bold and make mistakes. Just be open to learning from your mistakes.

10
SWITCH

Nowadays, wherever I go and whatever kind of roles/offers I receive, whether for a film or a small inaugural event, it involves a mother and a child theme. I receive many compliments from whomever I meet, saying that I am an ideal mom for all the moms of today's generation. I have not tried to be the one, as I know that no mother/father can be perfect; we have to be fully available for our kids no matter what. That is all I am doing. And, of course, it takes a lot of effort and energy. The first couple of years after my delivery, I didn't step out of the house; I didn't depend on any nanny or help, except for my parents and my husband's support, which is their duty and responsibility. This truly helps in building a bond with the child. I even started exercising/thinking of losing some extra weight I had gained during pregnancy, only after I stopped breastfeeding my baby (precisely after two years since birth). Now that people appreciate my fitness and call me 'santoor mommy,' I can't deny but enjoy all the compliments I receive because I put effort into it. It is essential for any mother, especially to be fit and healthy (also helps mental health).

Previously, I recall I had finished shooting for a movie and was dubbing for it. In the dubbing process, I met one of my colleagues who was not yet a part of the film industry but was associated with one of my co-actors. This person is now very famous, but I met him earlier in his career. I didn't particularly appreciate meeting him because there was a vast difference in our opinions and attitudes toward life. We did not have friction back then, but I have observed his way of life for a long time. I could sense he had patriarchal views and was a male chauvinist. He has always had a male-centered approach toward everything in the industry. I met him again after he became successful and congratulated him on his upward journey. In the room full of people –many of whom were my colleagues – I was counted among the men in the industry who had gained weight. He was remarking on my post-pregnancy body weight. I was surprised to hear such an insensitive remark – he did not think twice before comparing my post-pregnancy body with men's! I do not see this as a stand-alone episode about body shaming; this and several such episodes have revealed his attitude toward women in general. One such "joke" can take women back and pull them out of their upward climb in their careers. I was distraught to know that a man with such views was famous in the Kannada Film Industry.

It is deeply upsetting to know that people with such limited views are in the public eye, reaping the benefits of success and exercising their influence over audiences. I genuinely hoped he was a better person than when we met at the dubbing studio. However, his insensitive remark about me becoming a new mother reminds me that it is still a man's world. I would have heartily accepted defeat if this was out of concern or to help me – no, his remark intended to compare me to men, of course, none of whom were ever to deliver a baby. People idolize this actor and reward him with government-recognized awards, and he has also achieved nationwide success. Still, his attitude and thoughts about women continue to be derogatory. As a professional woman, I do not take these differences personally. Still, I wonder about the fate of this industry if such powerful men have to be corrected at every instance.

This reminds me of my pregnancy – I was very concerned about my future in the business after having a baby. In our film industry, maternity leaves and pregnancy concerns are not formally incorporated into our contracts. It is unlike corporate jobs where women can exercise confident control over their opportunities even during pregnancy. Of course, one cannot compare because the corporate world has challenges. However, our Film Industry does not have an ideal attitude toward women and motherhood. Ours is a business where appearances matter – as much as the mind and the heart. I could be the most outstanding actor in the world. Still, without agility and a disarming screen presence, I would soon be forgotten from the screens. Developing a unique style and building an appearance that matches that style is essential.

Furthermore, when it comes to appearances, it is always more challenging for women than men. Women are born into a world where beauty standards are sky high – one where fair-skinned and skinny women continue to be the most desirable "item" of the industry. In such a competitive world, being an actor after giving birth to a baby comes with added pressures. Moreover, despite its nationwide achievements in the past few years, the regional film industry is limited in resources. Hence, industry professionals are tied to market expectations – unwilling to give opportunities to rather "unconventional actresses.' It is the need of the hour for us to eradicate these biases and give art the respect it deserves. Indeed, being a part of the film industry can be detrimental for women because so many odds are always against us. Being a mother entails being everything to everyone in the house. You are a planner to one, a cook to another, a counselor to another, a doctor to another, and so on.

Now that I am a mother, I was very concerned about the logistics of the projects I would take up. Not about the kind of roles I wanted to portray, but my child was a priority for me, something that can be considered a hindrance to others amidst the hustle and bustle of a film set. I didn't want to be a trouble to a producer or a director. So, I was evident with my conditions before signing a movie postpartum. At first, I signed 'Hope' because the film was to be filmed in Bengaluru. It was a massive help because I would not have to live apart from my daughter and continue to build my professional career. It makes me tremendously happy to know that the film is now available on over-the-top platforms – my labor of love is not general for all to watch at leisure! All thanks to such a fantastic team for understanding a mother's situation. Getting such a strong character role after becoming a mother was empowering.

This was rare in our Kannada/other regional film industry. This was a new mindset in the business. Kudos to that. Of course, this good fortune would have to fade away someday. I have always aspired to do exciting projects that challenge me as an actor and help me propel my career. After 'Hope,' I got the massive opportunity to work on 'Raghavendra Stores.' I was thrilled to be offered a role from a prominent production house, 'HOMBALE", one of the biggest production houses in the country. This offer was crucial as I had a baby, and still, the proposal was for the lead role. I felt happy about myself as I didn't rush and signed the movie just because the offer was overwhelming; I took my time to understand the story and character and made my point to them about conditions as a mother before signing the movie.

I have been firm in my decisions since the beginning; I am picky about the characters that I play and the team I work with, and I was in a position where I didn't compromise on my monetary benefits. Of course, the debate regarding the male and female disparity/inequality in money/payouts is still ongoing. Still, now that we all understand the business, I was happy with what I was demanding for my work. I appreciate that such a big production house agreed to all my requirements for signing me for this film. It is a proud moment for an actress with a toddler. At this moment of uncertainty, my mother proved to be a savior as we traveled all over the state.

She agreed to embark upon the set journey with me upon my request. I would have to travel across multiple destinations in Karnataka for the film. Furthermore, I had to have my child with me throughout the filming because she was very young. Thankfully, the production team agreed to ensure the safekeeping and care of my mother and my daughter during the entire shoot. This is one of the most empowering practices of the Kannada film industry.

I was accepted for the role, and my motherhood was embraced by the team as well. Without the team's support, taking care of my child and mother would have been impossible. Moreover, I was astonished that a production house agreed to hire me with all my conditions. They could have hired anyone without situations like mine, yet they ensured I joined them and cared for all my needs. I am very grateful for such an effort to make me at home. Talent and experience help one build a dependable career.

With my actions and talents help, I gained enough significance for a big production house to take such intimate care of me and my loved ones while filming a project. After this experience, I was more confident in my abilities. Furthermore, how could this have been possible without the aid of my darling mother? She took the leap of faith for me, agreed to travel to unknown places for forty days, and cared for my toddler. Professional women need the support of their families; my mother was my anchor during my journey. If you wonder if a woman is behind a man's success – you are wasting time on a somewhat redundant question. Of course, men and women work towards creating egalitarian relationships.

However, for a married woman and a new mother, her mother is the guide and mentor she needs. Despite her troubles, I am grateful that my mother joined me for this film shoot. She has had several major surgeries and has to push herself in instances of physical exertion.

However, regarding my career and professional choices, she did not bat an eyelid and agreed to join me. No doubt, the opportunity came my way because of my hard work and previous experience in the industry; I would not have benefited from the opportunity had I not had my mother by my side. Despite the freshness of this wholesome experience, I cannot deny the past. Getting her has taken me a considerable amount of time, and rewarding opportunities are finally coming my way. In the past, I would seldom have to pull myself out of the most stubborn rut and begin anew. Furthermore, these mother duties would often be extended to me growing up. I was an elder child and a daughter – I was told I was responsible for my younger brother. Growing up, my role in his life was to be there for him and look after him.

Today, I love him unconditionally and feel very protective towards him. However, I was not entirely okay with this unequal expectation as a child. My family had a very different approach toward parenting and visualizing his future because he was a boy. Bound by gender roles, they had certain expectations of me as a girl that differed from those of my brother. Moreover, he had more ground to make mistakes; he was approached with leniency. Society tends to encourage men to be courageous and ambitious, challenging the heights of their success. On the other hand, women are expected to spend their time building a comfortable cushion they can fall onto when things get complicated. I was not ready to accept such a limited role in my own life. It was not because I loved my brother or my family any less. Their love and care had given me the wings to fly high – above and beyond the limits of my existence. I thought my mother could do better than listen to my father and accept his words as the ultimate truth. However, with time, especially after becoming a wife and a mother, I understood where she came from. I believed all the injustices she suffered were her fault. I learned later that there was a lot to consider before creating such a narrative in my heart. She was an individual – a product of her upbringing, education, personality, and core values.

Of course, they had to be different from mine! She grew up in a lower-middle-class family and a large family. She was among nine siblings and always at the receiving end of scattered attention. These experiences shaped how she looked at the world and herself. This, in turn, affected how she raised my brother and me thirty-five years ago.

Despite the problems she faced growing up, she has only expressed unconditional love for her family. My mother and my father loved their families despite issues in their upbringing. It was a value system that dictated their life, eventually permeating how they viewed their marriage and parenting style. For them, respect was the highest form of love; it was the respect that sustained their marriage.

Today, parenting is viewed as a complex and subjective experience – full of ups and downs where parents and children converse about their expectations and beliefs. I stand in between this transition in human history – hence, over time, I have attempted to retain the love and respect my parents had for each other; at the same time, I wish to make the most of the resources I have had and build a professional career of my own, a family of my own. Of course, things may look different from how families and parents are today.

As much as we would like to build happy and healthy relationships, sometimes, material realities take over all our sensibilities. Growing up, standing on our feet, and making sure our home was unbreakable amidst the storm of economic upheavals or personal failures was most important, unlike today, where my partner and I are climbing a social ladder, cementing our place at a unique place where we can afford to spend time towards building our family.

Moreover, as I have reiterated, reflection helps us look within ourselves. It is a positive tool that can enable us to untie the knots within us and evolve. One must not hold on to negative experiences. Instead, we must observe our reactions and impulses in such moments and attempt to do better. My experience as a mother in the film industry has witnessed a trajectory unlike any other. From not worrying about my appearance after my pregnancy to being ushered with my mother and daughter for a big-budget movie recently – artists and audiences have revealed diverse responses to my journey. I am delighted to share them as a word of consolation and a word of caution for more women like me in the world!

Every day, I wake up and thank my stars for being loved by my fans, who are here to listen to my stories and struggles. People with similar experiences or in the same field will acknowledge the presence of bias and the effort that comes with it. There are so many women out there who have helped us to be where we are today … hats off to all those people, women and men, who have fought for women's rights, which are human rights. They are the inspiration. Education, awareness, knowledge … these are the aspects we should fill our minds with. Only these things help us excel in our battles. Make it possible, ladies. Who runs the world? Girls…

11
QUESTIONS AND ANSWERS

My audience, well-wishers, and fans mean abundance to me. Language does not contain a word intense enough to express my feelings. They keep me humble, motivated and inspired. They have been the driving force and reason for me to be a part of the movie industry through every hurdle I have crossed and will have to in the future. I have devoted much of my time writing this book as a token of appreciation and love to my audience. However, while writing this book, the narrative hugely focuses on my life from my perspective. It includes stories from my childhood, my journey in the film industry, and so much more. Still, I was unaware of what people wanted to know about me. I was curious about their questions and perspectives of me, and that is when I decided to conduct a Q and A session with them. While going through these questions, I discovered that there are specific things that people want to learn about me and that some of these things also need to be addressed in the book. Hence, this chapter.

1. Why do only men rule the Kannada industry?

Men dominate every industry and tend to be the center focus. These problems become more significant when the market is smaller. To better understand this, let me put it this way. Media influences power people, and more often than not, men have been given the pedestal to make more ticket sales and money for the people behind the art. This stems from the belief that men do this better due to gender dominance. However, even though we are here to make art, most want to make a fat cheque. Art and money become linear and blend. And that is poached by enabling male dominance in the industry.

2. After Kiragoorina Gayyaligalu, you took a break. Why is that? Is it because of marriage or no offers?

Making a movie is a tedious journey; making one that takes about 2.5 hours takes an entire village and all resources. The filming is often done in remote locations for months, including adapting to the character we are playing. Everything is a matter of monetary benefit in the industry; dealing with people looking to make money becomes an everyday task. As such, art and representation in the industry take a back seat when money comes to light. However, I have a moral I set for myself as an artist; I am more sensitive, disciplined, and principled. I am passionate about what I do, and money has never been a concern or deciding factor. Having other people deal with finances while I take a break to rejuvenate after completing a project is advisable. After all, as a woman, I have multiple roles to play as a wife, mother, and daughter apart from my reel world.

3. You have touched many bases, like movies, dance, music, travel, health, and family. What keeps you motivated and jovial?

I have garnered some good life skills through my journey. A lot of which stems from having a positive outlook and loving myself. That is essential, as I would have given up quickly had it not been for my go-with-the-flow nature. Accepting every challenge that comes my way is a conscious choice I make to live life to the fullest. Otherwise, I traverse every human emotion like the rest of us.

I choose to hold no grudges and go my own way. All of these keep me motivated and cheerful.

4. Many women who want to enter the film industry have undergone physical and sexual harassment. What advice would you like to give?

Many biopics of female actors in the past have discussed this topic in great detail. I have heard several such stories of harassment from a few people in the industry. Sadly, women with aspirations who want to enter the industry have often been subjected to these shameful and heinous acts. A few men in the industry approached me with specific intentions. Still, I had the privilege to choose for myself and refrained from going down that path. When I struggled to make a name for myself in the industry as a rookie, I was already married, which made many men hesitant to talk to me; most rejected me. My advice to all the young girls who want to enter the industry and make a name for themselves is do not go down this path; I promise you that it's not worth it. The people who approach you with wrong intentions will not help you get where you aspire to be. If it is meant to be, it will happen if you are destined to make a name for yourself in this industry. It might take some time, but it will happen, so believe in yourself, work hard, and do not get discouraged by rejections. But never trust someone's empty promises.

5. How would you handle failure in life?

At this juncture in my life, I question what success and failure mean. However, the same has not been the case in the past when I was young; dealing with failure was disappointing, and I would question myself and lose confidence. I've always had my parent's support, but you must seek it to achieve your goals. Hustling is an imminent process to reach your goal. Still, the same can be accomplished when you allow yourself to make mistakes. Every fall will enable a different lesson; the sooner you acknowledge it, the easier life becomes to navigate.

6. What are the best moments your parents witnessed in your life?

This answer may have been different had I not been experiencing parenthood. This may be very cliche, but from a parents' perspective, we are the happiest when we see our children achieve their goals. Nobody prepares you for parenthood, and with the rapid global changes, it's impossible to have linear and binary parenting. However, everything boils down to wanting to see your kids gain their accomplishments, protecting them, guiding them, and being their pillar of support. We always want to see our kids secure. Similarly, when I attained my dream and reached a place of contentment, it made me joyous and became the best moment for my parents; they derived their happiness through mine.

7. Please share decision-making ideas…

Every individual's decision-making process is unique; I choose to discuss my decisions with my safety net to give myself a clear conscience. Before I take any step, I assess its pros and cons and talk about whether I am physically and mentally capacitated to face it. Everything has a best and worst course for a decision, and having clarity about it might occur much later, but that shouldn't be a deterrent from taking the step. If you embrace that, you will better know what you want.

8. Why did you struggle in the film industry when you had money and fame?

To clarify this, I want to state that there is a presumption that I do not come from a middle-class life. Due to this, their respect, compassion, and empathy for my struggles and wins were reduced. People must understand that I may be an actor. Still, I am from the

Kannada industry, a small market with few opportunities for women. We barely see cinemas that talk about women, their views, and their perspectives. As an artist, I find films such as these to be of the utmost pleasure, and I strive to be a part of them. I am grateful to receive love from my fans.

I've always been asked not to stay caught up on what is monetary; money has always been a secondary priority. My parents have always believed that chasing one's dreams must be a priority and should be achieved through one's passion and will. People think I've climbed this ladder easily, but I've had no support to get where I am today. My life may appear glamorous now, but the same didn't happen when I tried to make it in the industry. To quote an incident, when I conceived, my parents were constructing a home in a posh residence; it was normal for us to stroll outside in the evenings. On one such evening, another family was on a stroll too; they approached me and praised my work, and insisted that we visit them as neighbors from now on, and we obliged. However, in the days to come, as our neighbors saw our house being completed, their behavior toward us changed. Our house wasn't extraordinary; it was a simple house filled with much love. It was what my father could afford.

People treat you differently based on what you show them; many people portray their lifestyle to be viewed appealingly by society. This lifestyle leads to nothing more than constantly having to be frustrated people pleasers sinking in debt. I find it wise to be true to yourself; I've grown up with ideologies that have always enabled me to view people equally and solely analyze them through their character and personality.

9. Why do married women or women with children struggle to return to their professional careers?

It is always advisable to take breaks, especially if one has to venture into a new relationship.

Parents and siblings are people you are born to. In contrast, spouses and children come into life much later, so adjusting takes some time, especially after becoming a mother, a woman's center of attention and priority in life changes. There are other medical and hormonal reasons why women hesitate to return to the workspace. As an actor, while we are pregnant, we cannot appear on the screen due to the obvious reasons.

This is one of many reasons women struggle to make a comeback. Society is formulated in a way that does not accommodate women who want to pursue a career and a family simultaneously. For example, in the film industry, women are suggested not to get married or have children. I was asked not to disclose my marital status to the media until much later. This is mainly because women in the film industry are considered objects of desire. Married women and mothers cannot come under the "subjective desire" category as commonly seen in the film storyline. Hence, casting directors and producers are hesitant to cast an actor who also happens to be a mom or a wife.

10. What was your journey in the film industry after your marriage?

This is a major question I have been asked earlier by the media and people associated with me. I was married to my dear husband before entering the film industry. I am so thankful that he supported me mentally and often accompanied me to meet producers or casting directors when I started in the industry. He backed my dreams and pushed me to pursue them when I sometimes felt like giving up. So, most of the struggles I faced were after marriage and frequently because of my marriage.

11. Do you ever feel uncomfortable when filming intimate or kissing scenes?

This question is very different, and thinking about it makes me giggle. Married actors must talk with their partners and create an extra special understanding.

Whether before or after marriage, any girl or guy will feel awkward kissing or being intimate with someone with whom they have no romantic relationship. Not only that, when we are filming, about fifty to sixty people are a part of the film crew; there are also technicians, junior actors, and many other contributors.

With so many eyeballs around watching you, it is not easy to surrender your physical self to someone, and one must prepare oneself mentally before taking part in intimate scenes. Adding to this, we must remember the theme, the plot, the character's motif, mannerisms, etc., since we are acting. Actors are not supposed to have any inhibitions to perform effortlessly. Keeping all this in mind, actors don't have the time to feel uncomfortable while filming an intimate scene because we are trying to create a piece of art for the public to believe and act out a crucial part of the plot. How we handle ourselves in these situations adds to the film industry's reputation and defines us as actors.

12. When playing a part in a woman-centric movie, is it better to have a male or female director?

This question makes me very eager to reply since it makes me think. There will be a considerable gap between how men deal with stories about women and how women deal with the same. The story will be different because of how uniquely every woman deals with their experiences, no matter how observant you are or how the characters are fictional. It's about authenticity. It's about the point of view, psychology, and the energy that is different when it comes to directors. I have worked for female directors and producers. I feel happy that I got the opportunity to work with them. I feel a little more relaxed working with the opposite gender; these men are not very good at multitasking, but still, they know how to share their responsibilities with the whole team and crew. Men in this industry know how to give creative freedom to artists to do a successful project. This is not to say that female directors or producers do not do the same. Still, since they get an opportunity to make a movie after so many struggles, they tend to be particular about every minute detail, limiting my freedom as an artist. So, I feel despite gender, they have their own advantages and disadvantages in both cases. But in any case, I do not choose to be a part of a film because of the gender of the crew but because of the plot and the character.

13. Do you lose yourself to the character while playing a character?

This is an intense question. An actor needs to be extremely sensitive and have a high sense of empathy. Every time we play a character, we have to put ourselves in someone else's shoes; they might be a natural person or a fictional character; either way, we have to portray and be as authentic, respectful, and open-minded to their whereabouts as much as possible even though we might not relate to them. Senior artists often say that to be a good actor, one has to be a good human being. Before playing a character, an actor has to go through a rigorous process of research and workshops. During this extensive research and analysis process, we meet with people with similar experiences as the characters. Many actors go to extremes to get into and commit to the characters. Then, when the filming process starts, each scene is shorter and divided into several shots. Each time we give a shot, we have to get into character. When the shot is over, actors have to snap back to their real personalities to review the shot they have just given and to check if they are satisfied with the same. This is where the tricky part of being an actor lies. All that glitz and glamour portrayed by the media about our industry is a minimal ingredient. Being an actor is about constantly playing a psychological game; it is often very tiring, stressful, and depressing. We lose ourselves to the character, but it is very momentary because a part of our brain holds on to ourselves and reminds us that we are at work and this is our job. Ultimately, if you like what you are doing, no matter how hard it is, you will return to it and enjoy it.

14. Why have you done very few movies in the past 15 years? Aren't there many offers? Or are you being so choosey?

I can say the reason is actually both. There is not much scope for women as a lead protagonist, my marital status being the reason, and my bad PR skills, too. We need to be smarter and have more networks... a lot of qualities are required to be in the biz. As for my mentality, after finishing every movie, I am physically and mentally exhausted since making a movie is a tedious process, and it takes time to make a 2.5- or 3-hour movie. Then, we give our energy to just the character we are portraying, deal with the different kinds of mentality, and bow in front of hypocrites once we have signed a project. And every time I finish one project, I tell myself that I can't do this anymore. To make a movie, one has to deal with very business-minded people. The people in our industry first think of money and then think of art and representation.

Yet, as an artist, I am more sensitive, disciplined, and principled. I follow many strict morals in life, and that is how I was raised. Most importantly, I am in the movie business because I am passionate about acting and being on the screen, and I know my worth... I choose from what I get, so I do less work, and I try to give quality work.

15. Why is it that age factor and parenthood don't matter for male lead actors, and it affects only women in films and any other careers? I am a working mother and have been following you since your TV serial days. I have observed in your

interviews that you have mentioned this in many talks shows. I thought I'd get an elaborate answer from your book.

Thank you for your kind words. It is really overwhelming to know that I have an audience and well-wishers who are keeping track of and following my work. It feels very sustaining to do what I think is right for me rather than blindly following the crowd.

I myself have thought about this a lot of times; in fact, these are the kinds of thoughts that provoked me to decide on taking up this career when I had a so-called 'settled life' with a secure career and when I was about to start my own family.

This gender bias has been embedded in our minds for a very long time. In just a couple of decades, our senior women citizens have started an effort to bring about change.

We have to ensure that we also take it forward and bring about that change of mindset amongst society in our own ways of fighting for our basic rights on our paths so that our future generation will at least not have to see this injustice. Yes, it will be a hell of a journey, with chaotic situations and rollercoaster rides, but it will definitely be worth it for our future generations.

I have shared in this book how I had to fight for my position in my movies in spite of being a married woman and a mother. Hopefully, you will agree with my words. Thank you for this wonderful question

www.ingramcontent.com/pod-product-compliance
Lightning Source LLC
Chambersburg PA
CBHW030001050426
42451CB00006B/79